B. H. Bristow

Trail and Camp-Fire

The Book of the Boone and Crockett Club

EDITORS
GEORGE BIRD GRINNELL
THEODORE ROOSEVELT

HARPER & BROTHERS, PUBLISHERS
NEW YORK & LONDON
MCMXIV

Contents

3

Contents

List of Illustrations

5

List of Illustrations

Preface

The third volume of the Boone and Crockett Club book is now presented to its members. The two earlier ones "American Big Game Hunting," and "Hunting in Many Lands," were published in 1893 and 1895, respectively, the purpose of the club being to issue one such volume every two years.

Since the publication of the last volume a wider public interest has been aroused in several of the objects for which the club is working, and not a little progress has been made· in carrying them out. Some of these matters deserve especial mention.

Late in the year 1895 the National Academy of Sciences, at the request of the Secretary of the Interior, appointed a committee of forestry experts, who should examine the national forests and report upon them. After this committee had reported, thirteen additional forest reservations in the West, covering 21,000,000 acres of land, were set aside by Presidential proclamation. This action was directly in the line of recommendations urged in the Boone and Crockett Club books, and two members of the club were appointed by the National Academy of Sciences as members of this committee.

More local, but still of the highest importance, is the successful setting on foot of the New York Zoological Society, the incorporation of which was mentioned in the club's previous volume. The history of the Society in some detail will be found in the following pages. The Boone and Crockett Club is largely represented on the board of management of the Zoological Society, and much of the Society's success is due to the unselfish energy of these members.

The abolition in the Adirondacks, for a period of five years, of the unsportsmanlike practices of driving deer to the water by hounds and of jack-lighting is to be credited largely to the efforts of the Boone and Crockett Club. The chairman of its game law committee spent much time in Albany working with the New York Legislature to bring about the passage of this bill, and a member of the club, who was also a member of the

Preface

Legislature, introduced and carried through the measure which put an end to this slaughter. A paper from the pen of this member will be found in the present volume. For many years attempts had been made to stop hounding, and once a law forbidding it was enacted, but the influence of the hotels and of a certain portion of the Adirondack guides was too strong to be permanently overcome until the Boone and Crockett Club took hold of the matter.

In Captain Anderson's paper, in the club's last volume, entitled "Yellowstone Park Protection," the history of the destruction of the Park herd of buffalo was fully given, but the number of these animals remaining in the Park could only be conjectured. Recent estimates based on animals and tracks seen last winter, seem to justify the conclusion that the buffalo left alive there number between twenty-five and fifty. Probably there are between thirty and forty. They are badly scattered, and, even under the most favorable circumstances, their increase must be very slow.

The two earlier volumes of the club's publication, though devoted chiefly to accounts of hunting adventure, contain also considerable matter bearing on the natural history of North American game and forest preservation. In the present volume an effort is made to devote somewhat more space to the natural history side of our large animals, for the publications of the club should contain material of permanent value. Of course, any book, whether on hunting or science, should be interesting, but it should be something else, too. Hunting stories should be more than merely pleasant reading. The purposes of the club are serious, and its published papers should be of a lasting character. We would call special attention to Mr. Low's admirable paper on the Peninsula of Labrador, which is an abstract of his talk given before the club at its last annual meeting. The composite chapter on the habits of bears contains some material that is absolutely new, and additional contributions of this nature may confidently be looked for hereafter from members of the club. The big game hunter is a man who travels about with his eyes open, and the more familiar he is with the habits of game the greater will be his success. The best hunters owe their success less to their skill with the rifle than to the knowledge which they have acquired of the game

Preface

that they pursue, and the closer a man's habits of observation the more speedily will he become a good hunter.

In this volume will be found the draft of the new constitution, authorized at the club's annual meeting to be submitted for ratification at the coming one. The changes made in this are chiefly in the direction of raising the standard of the qualifications for membership, and in more, sharply defining the position taken by the club in matters of sport. Such changes cannot fail to appeal to most members, who will recognize that the Boone and Crockett Club cannot take too high ground in relation to all matters pertaining to its objects.

GEORGE BIRD GRINNELL.
THEODORE ROOSEVELT.

NEW YORK, October 1, 1897.

11

General Benjamin H. Bristow

From the Club Minutes of January 16, 1897

The chairman gave expression to the club's sense of loss in the death of the president, and it was voted that an entry be made in the minutes of the meeting, as follows:

General Bristow was a man who was distinguished in many walks of life. He was an accomplished lawyer, a brave soldier, a statesman pre-eminent for ability and integrity; he represented true American citizenship in its highest and best sense.

As a member and officer of the Boone and Crockett Club, General Bristow was devoted to the interests of the organization, and to the wider public interests with which it is concerned. By sentiment, influence and example he stood for what is highest and most worthy in sportsmanship. His membership in the club, his warm interest in its work, and his devotion as a presiding officer will be cherished in its annals as an abiding honor.

General Bristow was a singularly pleasant companion, and a most staunch and loyal friend. While it is fitting that the club should make note in its minutes of the loss of a member and officer whose death is deplored, no such formal record can express in any degree the regret and the keen sense of personal loss felt by all its members who knew him.

The Labrador Peninsula

In many minds the name Labrador is associated with the picture of a barren, rock-bound coast, continuously hidden by a thick veil of fog and mist, and lashed by the waves of the ice-laden North Atlantic; a land without redeeming features, barren, cold and uninhabited, except by a few degraded Eskimo who struggle for existence in this semi-polar region. To some extent this view is justified by the aspect of the northeastern coast, where the sweep of the arctic current bears southward throughout the summer a continuous stream of icebergs, which lower the temperature of the coastal region to such an extent as to prevent the growth of trees on the islands or exposed portions of the coast. The unknown interior was supposed to be of a similar character, and only during the past few years has sufficient knowledge been gained to refute such ideas, and to show that, although by no means a country fit for agriculture throughout, it is much less barren and desolate than was formerly supposed.

Trail and Camp-Fire

The distinction of being the earliest discovered and latest unknown portion of the American continent may be claimed for the Labrador Peninsula. In 990 A. D. Biarne, the Norseman, sailed from Greenland and skirted the shores of Labrador on his voyage southward, probably to Nova Scotia. He was followed by other crews of these adventurers, whose latest voyage to America was in 1347. After a lapse of one hundred and fifty years Labrador was rediscovered by John Cabot in 1497, on a voyage from Bristol in search of a passage westward to Cathay. About the same time the fisheries of Labrador and Newfoundland became known to the Basque fishermen, and in 1504 the town of Brest was founded on the north side of the Strait of Belle Isle. This town grew rapidly, so that in 1517 over fifty vessels called there; and at the height of its prosperity, about 1600, Brest contained 200 houses, and a population of about 1,000 persons.

Mercator's map of 1569 shows the coasts of Labrador and Ungava, or Hudson Bay, and, as he derived his information from Portuguese sources, it is evident that the fishermen of that country had previously penetrated Hudson Strait. The search for a northwest passage to China brought to the coast of Labrador Martin Frobisher in 1577, John Davis in 1586, Weymouth in 1602, and finally, in 1610, Henry Hudson, who discovered the great bay called after him.

In 1603 Champlain established Quebec, and shortly afterward the Jesuit missionaries began their labors among the Indians, traveling through the northern interior from camp to camp, and incidentally gaining a knowledge of the country. The hardy *couriers des bois.* or French trappers, also soon overran the northern wilds, where they acquired the habits of the natives, and usually took to themselves wives from among the Indian friends. Much of the knowledge gained from these sources was, incorporated in Delisle's map of 1703 which shows the principal lakes and rivers, especially of the southern and eastern watersheds of the peninsula, in marked contrast to the lack of detail found in English maps of the same period used in the delineation of the boundaries between the territories of England and France as laid down by the Treaty of Utrecht in 1713.

The Hudson Bay Company was formed in 1669, and within a few years had several posts established at the mouths of rivers flowing into Hudson Bay, where for many years they confined their trade without attempting to explore inland; and it was not until after the formation of their rival, the Northwest Company, in about 1760, that they were forced to establish posts inland. Long before that date the French had trading posts scattered throughout the northern interior from the Gulf of St. Lawrence westward to the foot of the Rocky Mountains. After the amalgamation of the Northwest Company with the Hudson Bay Company in 1821, the following trading posts were for a time maintained in the interior of the peninsula: Waswanipi, Mistassini, Temiscamie, Metiskin, Nichicun, Kaniapiskau, Fort Nascaupee, Michikamau and Winokapau. Of these at present only Waswanipi, Mistassini and Nichicun remain. The officers and servants of the company employed at these posts must have had a good knowledge of the interior of the peninsula, but, until quite lately, it was the policy of the company to give no information to outsiders, and, in consequence, all such knowledge has been lost. The only officer of the company who left a written account of his journeys through Labrador was

The Labrador Peninsula

John McLean,* who resided at Fort Chimo on Ungava Bay, and made several trips through the interior from there to Hamilton Inlet between 1838 and 1840, on the way discovering the grand falls of the Hamilton River.

The first exploration undertaken by the Canadian government was that of H. Y. H. Hind in 1862. He ascended the Moisie River some 200 miles; and from his observations and information obtained from Indians and others wrote two large volumes, which until quite recently were the standard authority on matters relating to the Labrador Peninsula. In 1870 and 1871 parties were sent out by the Geological Survey to explore the country between Lake St. John and Lake Mistassini, and in 1884, owing to the absurd rumors as to the immense size of Lake Mistassini, an expedition was organized to complete the survey of the lake. I was attached as geologist to the party, and in the spring of 1885 was promoted to the charge of the expedition. We completed the survey of the lake, finding it, as was expected, about 100 miles long, much to the disgust of the enthusiasts who, on the strength of Indian stories, had claimed that it

*Twenty-five Years in the Hudson Bay Territory.

was equal to, if it did not exceed, the size of Lake Superior. On the completion of the survey of Lake Mistassini I descended its outlet, the Rupert River, to James Bay, and returned home by ascending the Moose River to the Canadian Pacific Railway north of Lake Superior.

In 1887 and 1888 I was employed on exploratory work among the islands of James Bay and on the rivers flowing into the east side of Hudson Bay. In 1887 R. F. Holmes attempted to reach the Grand Falls of the Hamilton River by ascending the river from its mouth, but, owing to lack of proper equipment and a poor crew, was obliged to return without accomplishing his purpose. On his return to England he published an account of his trip in the Transactions of the Royal Geographical Society. Arguing from the elevation of the interior plateau as given by Hind, and from the height of the river below the falls, he arrived at the conclusion that the total fall must be about 2,000 feet, and inferred that it was all made in a single jump.

In 1891, fired by Holmes' account, two separate expeditions started from the United States to discover the falls, and both reached

The Labrador Peninsula

them within a few days of each other. To Austin Cary and D. M. Cole,* of the Bowdoin College expedition, fell the honor of first arrival. Unfortunately they burnt their boat and outfit, and were obliged to tramp and raft down stream 250 miles to the mouth of the river. On their way down they passed unseen Henry G. Bryant† and C. A. Kenaston, who were on their way up. These latter made a careful determination of the falls, finding the drop to be slightly over 300 feet, and thus shattered the belief in another of the marvelous wonders of unknown Labrador.

In 1892 I was sent to explore the East Main River, which flows westward, close to the fifty-second parallel, into Hudson Bay, to determine its suitability for a natural boundary between the Province of Quebec and the northern territories of the Dominion. I ascended the Ashouapmouchouan River from Lake St. John to the Height of Land, passed through Lake Mislaosiori and proceeded northward about 100 miles to the East Main River, and followed it downward some 300 miles to

*Bull. Am. Geog. Soc., Vol. XXIV.
†A Journey to the Grand Falls of Labrador. Geog. Club, Philadelphia.

its mouth. The following year in continuation
of the boundary work, I again reached the East
Main by the same route, and then ascended it
150 miles to its source; from there we crossed
several branches of the Big River, which also
flows into Hudson Bay, and so reached the
upper part of the southern branch of the
Koksoak River, and followed its course downward to Ungava Bay. From there we took
passage in the Hudson Bay Company's
steamer to Hamilton Inlet, where we passed
the early part of the winter at Northwest
River, a small post near its head.

In March, 1894, we started inland, hauling
on sleds, up the Hamilton River, outfit and
provisions sufficient for the next summer's
work. The quantity was so great that it required four trips to move it, and in consequence our progress was very slow—about
twenty-five miles a week. After considerable
hardship and trouble we succeeded in reaching
the neighborhood of the Grand Falls on the
19th of May, when the advent of spring soon
brought open water, and with it easier canoe
travel. During the summer we explored two
branches of the Hamilton River and Lake
Michikamau, which lies to the north at the

The Labrador Peninsula

head of the Northwest River, and which is second in size only to Lake Mistassini. In August we proceeded southward by way of the Romaine and St. John rivers, and reached the mouth of the latter at the end of the month, after an absence of sixteen months from civilization.

In 1895 I spent two months in exploring the country about the central area on the headwaters of the Manicougan River that flows into the Gulf of St. Lawrence, the Big River of Hudson Bay and the Koksoak of Ungava Bay. Last summer I made a trip across the northern part of the peninsula from Richmond Gulf on Hudson Bay to the mouth of the Koksoak River.

The results of the past five years explorations in conjunction with the previous work done in Labrador are sufficient to give a general idea of the physical features and natural resources of the peninsula; and there only remains an area of about 100,000 square miles in the northwestern part totally unknown, but even this will be partly explored during the coming summer (1897) by the expedition to be sent out in May to Hudson Strait and thence to work southward.

The outline of the peninsula is roughly that of a right-angled triangle, the base being a line drawn from the foot of James Bay eastward to where it reaches the north shore of the Gulf of St. Lawrence, in the neighborhood of latitude 50 degrees, and from there following the coast to the Strait of Belle Isle. The perpendicular, which is about the same length as the base, or 1,000 miles, is represented by the coast fronting on Hudson Bay, which runs nearly north and south; the remaining side is formed by the coast line facing the Atlantic and Hudson Strait, and, owing to the great jog caused by Ungava Bay, has a length of nearly 2,000 miles. The total area of the peninsula is nearly 550,000 square miles, or equal to one-sixth of the area of Canada or the United States. The southern part of this vast territory belongs to the Province of Quebec, the East Main and Hamilton rivers being the natural boundary between the Province and Ungava District on the north belonging to the Dominion. A strip of coast extending from the Strait of Belle Isle to Cape Chidley at the eastern entrance of Hudson Strait is under the jurisdiction of the government of Newfoundland.

The Labrador Peninsula

Labrador may be considered as a plateau, which, except in a few places, rises abruptly from the coast to a general elevation of 1,500 feet above sea level, while the central area has a general elevation of nearly 2,000 feet. This plateau has an undulating surface, broken by ranges of rocky hills that rise from 400 feet to 800 feet above the general level, while minor ridges of glacial drift, from 50 feet to 200 feet high, also break the general contour. The wide, irregular valleys between these ridges are covered with innumerable lakes that vary in size from great bodies of water 100 miles long to mere ponds. The lakes are connected by networks of streams, so that with a knowledge of the country a journey in almost any direction may be made with canoes without portages exceeding two or three miles in length, and, as a rule, less than half a mile long. There are four principal watersheds; the western, with its rivers flowing into Hudson Bay, is the greatest; next in area is the northern, followed by the southern, and the last is the eastern, where, with the exception of the large rivers emptying into Hamilton Inlet, no streams of importance occur, owing to a high coastal range which throws most of the drainage to the northward. Toward their heads the rivers flow nearly on a level with the surrounding country without definite valleys, but as they approach the coast they descend into deep valleys, which they follow to the sea. The Saguenay is an example of one of these valleys, cut down 1,500 feet below the level of the surrounding country, while the valley of the Hamilton extends 400 miles inland, and is everywhere several hundred feet below the general level.

As might be expected with a range of 1,000 miles in latitude, there are great differences in climate between the southern and northern portions of Labrador. Along the shore of the Gulf of St. Lawrence hardy crops are easily grown, and many of the river-valleys are well fitted for settlement. As the central area is approached the climate becomes more rigorous, and varies from temperate in summer to extreme cold in winter, when the thermometer often registers 50 degrees below zero. Along the coast of Hudson Bay good root crops are raised at Fort George in latitude 54 degrees, but on the Atlantic coast the summer temperature is so lowered by the ice-laden arctic current that only at the heads of the long fiords can vegetables be grown in the open air.

The southern watershed, south of latitude 52 degrees, is generally well wooded, and on the central plateau black spruce, larch and white birch grow, but they are generally very small. After passing northward of latitude 52 degrees the summits of the hills become bare, and continuing northward the barren areas increase, so that in latitude 55 degrees only small, stunted trees are found about the low margins of lakes and water-courses, while beyond latitude 58 degrees the conifers cease to grow, and small arctic willows and birches alone are met with.

The interior is inhabited during the winter by a few families of Indians belonging to the Algonquin or Cree family. They are divided into three tribes, the Montagnais of the south, the Nasacaupees of the northern interior and the coastal tribe of Hudson Bay. During the summer nearly all descend to the Hudson Bay posts on the coasts to trade and to meet their relatives and friends; and they usually remain at the coast from one to three months.

The Eskimo are found scattered along the coast from Hamilton Inlet to Hudson Strait

and down the east coast of Hudson Bay to
Fort George. The west branch of the Koksoak River, which closely parallels latitude
58 degrees, forms the dividing line between
the hunting grounds of the Eskimo and the
Indians in the interior; south of this line the
Eskimo confine themselves to the coast. Although no longer at war, there is no love lost
between these races, and they rarely associate
and never intermarry.

Travel in the interior of Labrador is confined to canoes in summer and to walking in
winter. Notwithstanding Gilbert Parker, who
sends a man across Labrador from Ungava on
a well-beaten trail, it is impossible to travel on
foot except when the streams and lakes are
frozen, on account of the long, irregular bays
of lakes that stretch out in all directions, as
well as the many deep, mossy swamps which
occupy the lower grounds when lakes are
absent. Pack animals cannot be used because
of the lack of fodder, the southern country
being deeply covered with moss, while the
northern barrens are clad with a mantle of
white lichens with little or no grass. The frequent portages put the use of heavy boats out
of the question, and reduce the modes of sum-

mer travels to canoes only. The Indians and
Hudson Bay Company use bark canoes, but
my experience is that a cedar canoe is much
better, as it carries more in proportion to size,
paddles and poles easier and faster, is much
more easily mended, and does not constantly
leak, and is but little heavier than a bark canoe.
Of course, much depends on the model of the
canoe, the ordinary straight, shallow, paddling
canoes of civilization being simply an abomina-
tion on long trips.

In winter, dogs are used on the coast, but
owing to the lack of convenient stores of food,
they cannot be employed in the interior for any
extended time, as a dog can only haul sufficient
food to last him two weeks, and in the depth
of winter, when the going is heavy, his effective
load would be much less. The barren-ground
caribou has not been used for hauling, and so
winter transport in the interior must be done
by men. In the winter, when the snow is
deep, a long, narrow toboggan is used, and the
load is about 200 pounds; in the cold, short
days ten miles may be taken to be a good
day's travel and I know of no harder work
than hauling such a load over the gritty snow,
in which the sleighs stick and must be hauled

by main strength up and down hill alike. In the spring, when the sun and rain has formed a crust on the snow, the toboggans are exchanged for sleds, and the going is much easier, so that a man can without great difficulty haul a load of 300 pounds twenty-five miles in a day. A serious hindrance to extended travel is caused by the absence of any assured supplies in the interior, especially during the summer, when the small Hudson Bay posts are absolutely without supplies of any kind, and when the few people remaining at them depend wholly on the fish caught in nets from day to day. Game and fish, although not scarce, cannot be depended on, and a full supply of food must be taken from the coast to escape the chance of starvation. Of course, if time is no object, stops might be made where fish or game are abundant, and a store of dried provisions laid in, but for constant travel no dependence can be placed on the game to supply the daily wants of a moderately large party.

In the following notes on the game of Labrador I have attempted to give what information I can, of interest to the sportsman, in regard to the distribution and habits of the various species, leaving out much that is of value only to the naturalist, and therefore somewhat foreign to the purpose of this paper.

As a region for big game the Labrador Peninsula may not compare favorably with the great game preserves of Africa or Asia, and many better hunting grounds may be found in the West and Northwest; but, although not a sportsman's paradise, there are many places where good bags may be made, especially in the barren and semi-barren lands of the northern interior.

Following the natural order, the wolf (*Canis lupus,* Linn.) is the first of the game animals met with in Labrador. For some unaccountable reason wolves are rarely met with anywhere in Labrador, even where the great herds of barren-ground caribou afford easy prey. In the more southern regions the scarcity of caribou may account for the few wolves found there, few skins being traded at the Hudson Bay posts, and I have never seen or heard a wolf during my journeys through the interior.

The arctic wolf (*Canis lupus,* var. *albus*) is also only occasionally taken in the barren grounds, and does not appear to enter the timbered regions of the interior.

The fox (*Vulpes vulgaris,* Fleming) is common throughout the peninsula, from the Gulf of St. Lawrence to the shores of Hudson Strait. The red, cross and silver or black foxes are only color varieties of the same species, as on the Moose River I found a litter containing two red, three cross and two black kittens, showing that the color no more constitutes varieties than does the difference of color in a litter of the kittens of the common cat. In the northern regions there appears to be a larger proportion of dark-colored and more valuable foxes than in the south.

The arctic fox (*Vulpes lagopus,* Linn.) occurs abundantly in the barren ground and southward to Nichicun. Along the seaboard they range further southward, descending to the southern part of James Bay, and on the Atlantic coast are plentiful about Hamilton Inlet, and more rarely southward to the Strait of Belle Isle, on their migrations during the winter from the north.

The barren-ground bear (*Ursus arctos,* Rich.) is undoubtedly found in the barrens of Labrador, as skins are brought in at intervals to Fort Chimo when the Indians have a favorable chance of killing it. On other occasions they leave it alone, having a great respect and fear for its ferocity and size. While descending the south branch of the Koksoak River in 1894 we saw tracks along the banks which my Indians said were much larger than those of any black bear they had ever seen; unfortunately we did not get sight of the animal.

The black bear (*Ursus americanus*, Pallas) is found everywhere in the wooded country, and a few are killed in the semi-barrens as far north as latitude 56 degrees. During August and September bears are commonly met with in the valleys of any of the southern rivers where there are extensive burnt areas covered with blueberries, on which the bears feed and grow fat. I have followed several of these streams, and I have never failed to see several bears. Assured sport may be obtained on a trip up any of the rivers emptying into the St. Lawrence, but probably the best place for bear hunting is in the valley of the Hamilton River, below the Grand Falls. The food conditions are perfect, and, as the upper part of the valley is not hunted by the Indians, the bears are very plentiful, and a good bag would undoubtedly be made there in the early autumn.

The polar bear (*Thalassarctos maritimus,* Linn.) as a rule is confined to the coast, and goes inland only in the early spring to produce its young. At such times it is met with from twenty-five to fifty miles inland. It is not common on the Atlantic coast, owing to the number of fishermen from Newfoundland who pass the summer there engaged in the cod fishery. These people kill all the bears that stray southward on the ice in summer, and prevent any breeding along the coast. To the northward of the cod fishery, in Hudson Strait, polar bears are common, and great numbers are annually killed by the Eskimo. The Hudson Bay Company's ships on their passage through the Strait usually get several among the ice. The most accessible place for polar bears is the outer islands of James Bay, where the animals are seldom hunted. In this locality I killed four bears during the summer of 1887, besides seeing several others. Moose factory may be reached by a canoe trip of a week or ten days from the Canadian Pacific Railway, and arrangements for boats could be made with the Hudson Bay Company, so that the islands might be visited, and the round trip made in six or eight weeks, with almost a certainty of bagging bears, as well as of good sport with ducks and geese, which breed in large numbers on the islands.

The moose (*Alce americanus,* Jardine) is only found in the southwest portion of Labrador. It does not occur to the east of the Saguenay, and to the west of that river its northern limit hardly reaches to the southern boundary of the peninsula. Moose are found in the region between the St. Lawrence and Lake St. John, and westward about the tributaries of the St. Maurice and other streams flowing southward into the St. Lawrence and Ottawa rivers. They are most abundant about the headwaters of the Ottawa to the northward of Mattawa. The building of railways and the settlement of the country about Lake Temiscaming is driving the moose northward, so that for the past few years a number have been killed about the southern part of James Bay, where for many years previous none had been taken.

Woodland caribou (*Rangifer caribou,* Linn.) are found in the southern wooded part of the peninsula, ranging northward into the semi-barren regions, where they overlap the southern range of the barren-ground caribou. About twenty-five years ago caribou were very numerous on the southern and western watersheds, but owing to the enormous areas then swept by fire, the caribou were practically exterminated, either directly by the fire or indirectly from the ease with which they were hunted in the restricted areas of greenwoods by the Indians, whose southern hunting lands were destroyed, and who were obliged to hunt closely in order to exist. Within a few years the interior became almost wholly depleted of caribou, and then the Indians died in numbers from starvation owing to the failure to find deer. Within the past few years the caribou have been increasing throughout the interior, and they will probably soon again be quite numerous. At present probably the most satisfactory hunting grounds for woodland caribou are to be found in the southern country to the west of the Saguenay, including the Lake St. John, St. Maurice and Ottawa regions, or along the coast of the Gulf of St. Lawrence eastward to the Strait of Belle Isle, the caribou becoming most numerous toward the east.

The barren-ground caribou (*Rangifer groenlandicus,* Linn.) ranges in immense bands over

the barren and semi-barren lands. On the
Atlantic coast they are found as far south as
the Mealy Mountains, a high barren range
between Hamilton Inlet and Sandwich Bay;
to the northward they come out on the coast
between Hamilton Inlet and Nain during the
winter, and are then killed in great numbers
by the inhabitants. During the winter of
1895-96 upwards of 5,000 animals were slaughtered by the natives about Davis Inlet, and
more than half of them were left to decay in
the woods without removing even the skins.
From information obtained from the northern
Indians and my own observations there appear to be three principal bands of the barren-
ground caribou in northern Labrador. The
first and smallest passes the winter on the
coast of Hudson Bay and the immediate interior, passing northward in the summer to the
barren lands beyond Clearwater and Seal
lakes. The second band comes southward
during the fall, and winters in the valleys of
the Koksoak and its branches; the third band
is that already referred to as being found on
the Atlantic coast. During the summer this
band retreats to the highlands to the northward of Nain, and in September migrates

southward. In doing so it divides into about equal parts, one portion following the coast, the other passing inland and wintering in the partly wooded country about the headwaters of the Hamilton and Ungava rivers. There appear to be great fluctuations in the size of the bands, and at times they almost disappear for a number of years, as was the case with the Ungava band in 1892, when, after a year of great slaughter, the deer failed to return, and in consequence the Indians, who depend upon them for food and clothing, were reduced to such straits that upward of 175 persons died of starvation and exposure. I have found in the old journals of the Hudson Bay Company that similar calamities have happened two or three times during the present century, caused directly by the indiscriminate slaughter by the Indians, who either nearly exterminated the band, or, as they believe, frightened away the deer by the stench of the decaying bodies lying about everywhere. The destruction of the Indians follows that of the deer, and then the latter have a chance to increase, as in the case with the Ungava herd at present, where, after two or three years of practical disappearance, the increase is becoming quite marked. The best and easiest place to make a hunt for trophies is on the hills in the rear of Nain. Until the end of October a steamer runs up the coast every two weeks, and calls at Nain, where Eskimo guides may be obtained. In September the horns are perfect, and the bucks are beginning to be lively, but have not yet congregated into large bands, and consequently require some skill in hunting, which is not the case when the migrations take place, as then the poor animals may be shot down easily, and the sport resembles that of a slaughter-yard.

In closing the list of game animals of Labrador mention may be made of the fur-bearing animals, including the marten, weasel, ermine, mink, wolverine, otter, beaver, muskrat and the common and arctic hares, all of which afford large quantities of valuable furs, the fur of Labrador being superior to that of any other part of the American continent.

Ducks and geese afford good shooting along the coasts of Labrador, especially on the west coast fronting on James Bay, where the low shores and swampy, grass-covered flats serve as excellent feeding grounds. Inland, the absence of suitable food in the small lakes and ponds accounts for the scarcity of graminaceous ducks and geese.

The Canada goose is met with in summer on all the northern rivers and larger lakes, and affords exciting sport during the moulting season, when they cannot fly, and are chased in canoes and killed with the paddles. This, to be sure, cannot be called sport in its true sense, but it is great fun, and also provides a change of diet. Along the coasts the Canada goose is met with frequently, and it breeds in large numbers on the outer islands of James Bay.

The snow goose or wavies, until within a few years back, were killed by tens of thousands on Hudson Bay on their way to and from their breeding grounds in the far north, but the settlement of the northwest appears to have greatly reduced their numbers, so that the Hudson Bay posts on the bay can no longer depend upon salt goose as the principal article of food throughout the year.

The brant goose is shot in large numbers along the north shore of the Gulf of St. Lawrence in spring and autumn, but they are never seen elsewhere in Labrador, being unknown to the northern Indians. They must pass direct from the St. Lawrence to their breeding grounds north of Hudson Strait.

Swans breed on the Belcher Islands, a chain of large islands that lie about seventy-five miles off the east coast of Hudson Bay opposite to Great Whale River. These islands have not yet been visited by white men, but I have seen swan feathers from there with the Eskimo at Great Whale River.

Black, pintail and teal ducks are the most common species found about the shores of Hudson Bay, and the first two breed there in great numbers. In the interior the black duck only is found, and is uncommon, owing to the absence of proper feeding grounds. The fish-eating ducks are common on the coasts and in the interior, where they are represented by two species of mergansers, scoters, golden-eye, whistler and surf ducks, along with the common and red-breasted loon, while on the coast eider ducks are very numerous.

The grouse are represented by five species—the ruffed, Canada, sharp-tailed, willow and rock ptarmigan. The ruffed grouse is abundant throughout the southern interior, northward to Lake Mistassini and the Hamilton River. The Canada grouse is common to the edge of the barren grounds, or to latitude 57 degrees. On Hamilton Inlet they are very numerous in the late autumn, when they appear to migrate inland, and are then so tame that they are snared with a loop on the end of a stick, and when shot the charge consists of four or five grains of BB shot.

The range of the sharp-tailed grouse is confined to the shores and islands of James Bay, where it is known as the "pheasant." In 1887 I obtained a clutch of eggs of this bird at the mouth of the East Main River, and in 1892 shot a number of young birds near that place, while last year I procured skins of adults along the east coast to beyond Fort George in latitude 54 degrees. The inhabitants informed me that it was quite common along the coast, where it feeds on the different small fruits found there in abundance.

The willow ptarmigan breeds in astonishing numbers throughout the barren and semi-barren lands, and is found abundantly about the willow-covered banks of the northern lakes and streams. Being a free flyer it affords much better sport than the other grouse, which too often cannot be induced to fly when once treed. The willow ptarmigan pass southward into the wooded country during the winter, and are often plentiful during the season along the north shore of the Gulf of St. Lawrence. The southern migration depends on the state of the food supply in the north, and the birds only come south in great numbers when the willows are covered with snow, or the buds encased with a coating of frozen rain.

The rock ptarmigan is a smaller and more northern species, breeding in the most northern portion of the peninsula, and coming south only in the winter. Many of these birds breed on the north side of Hudson Strait and cross to the south shore in September, when large numbers alight on the ships then passing through the strait.

The wading birds are not plentiful inland, but are common about James Bay and along the Atlantic coast. Formerly curlew were killed in great numbers, both on Hudson Bay and on the Atlantic coast, but of late years they have decreased rapidly, for some unaccountable reason. The conditions in the north have not changed, and the decrease is probably due to slaughter on their wintering grounds in the south.

The Labrador Peninsula may not contain the quantity and variety of big and feathered game found in the west and northwest portions of the continent, but no apologies are needed for its game fish, which are unrivalled anywhere.

The salmon fishing of the rivers flowing into the Gulf of St. Lawrence on its north side is famous the world over, while the land-locked salmon, lake and brook trout of the interior waters afford sport that cannot be surpassed.

The Atlantic salmon (*Salmo salar*) is found in all the rivers from the Saguenay eastward to the Strait of Belle Isle, thence northward along the Atlantic coast to Hudson Strait, and for about 100 miles down the east coast of Hudson Bay. The fishing of the Gulf is too well known to require any comment here, and I will confine my remarks to the salmon fishing of the eastern and northern rivers. The Atlantic coast under the jurisdiction of the government of Newfoundland has never been officially protected, and the cod fishermen have been allowed to use trap nets indiscriminately, the result being the almost total ruin of the salmon fishery, which only a few years ago equalled or surpassed that of the Canadian coast. In Hudson Strait, beyond the ravages of the cod-trap, salmon are still abundant, and the Hudson Bay Company make profitable net fisheries in the lower part of the George, Whale and Koksoak rivers of Ungava Bay. The Eskimo say that the rivers of the strait, to the westward of the Koksoak and for about 100 miles down to the east coast of Hudson Bay, are plentifully stocked with salmon. Along the north shore of the Gulf of St. Lawrence the fish strike into the river early in June; they are taken in Hamilton Inlet in July, but they do not ascend the Koksoak and other rivers of Ungava Bay until the middle of August. There appears to be some connection between the time that the fish strike into the rivers and the temperature of the water along the coast, the northern waters remaining cold longer than those about the southern coasts.

The landlocked variety of *Salmo salar* or *ouinaniche* (diminutive of *winan,* the Cree word for salmon) is found in Lake St. John and the tributaries of the Saguenay, where it has free access to the sea; but as the fish is found plentifully in both branches of the

Hamilton River above the Grand Falls, as well as in Lake Michikamau and the headwaters of all the rivers of the central plateau, except those of the western watershed, without any possible communication with salt water, I have no doubt that the *ouinaniche* represents the original salmon, a fresh-water fish, and that the Atlantic salmon has for some reason acquired an anadromous habit, like the sea-trout variety of *Salvelinus fontinalis,* the common brook trout. Wherever found the *ouinaniche* exhibits the game qualities which have made it so famous in the Lake St. John region. It never grows to the size of its sea-going brother, and rarely exceeds eight pounds in weight, being more often from two to four pounds. Good sport may be had with this fish on the Upper Hamilton River, at Lake Michikamau, on the Romaine and Manicougan rivers of the St. Lawrence, and on all the rivers of Ungava Bay.

Hearne's salmon, or the Arctic salmon, is found in the lower parts of all the rivers from Cape Jones, at the entrance to James Bay, northward through Hudson Strait and southward along the Atlantic to south of Nachvak. This fish is not a salmon, but a small-scaled

trout, quite distinct from the southern sea
trout, which is only an anadromous variety of
the brook trout (*Salvelinus fontinalis*). It
swarms in the mouths of all the northern
rivers, which it enters early in the summer. It
rises readily to a fly, and when hooked jumps
well and is very game. The weight varies
from two to fifteen pounds, the average being
about seven pounds, and altogether it is a
valuable addition to the eastern game fish.
Last year I brought home skins of this fish,
and they are at present in the hands of Pro-
fessor Prince, of the Marine and Fisheries
Department.

The brook trout (*Salvelinus fontinalis*) is
found in all the streams and lakes of the interior, and in many places ranges to six or seven
pounds in weight. The heavy fish are usually
found in the lakes and moderate-sized rivers;
those of the smaller streams usually vary in
weight from a half to two pounds, and more
than make up in quantity for the lack in
weight. In the very large rivers only small
fish are caught, probably owing to the large
fish congregating in deep pools away from the
shores. When all places are so favorable it is
hard to name any particular locality for brook

trout, but I think that the very best fishing is found on the Hamilton River above the Grand Falls, and from there to the heads of both branches of the river. In every rapid and eddy fish varying from four to seven pounds may be caught in unlimited numbers.

The lake trout (*Salvelinus namaycush*) abounds in all the lakes and in the larger rivers before they leave the level of the central area and descend into their deep valleys. The average weight of this fish is about eight pounds, but individuals up to thirty-five pounds are often taken by deep trolling, set lines or nets in the larger lakes. Good fishing with the fly is often found under patches of foam in eddies, but the fish as a rule are sluggish, and do not take freely, and when caught do not afford nearly as much sport as the landlocked salmon or brook trout.

The common whitefish (*Coregonus clupei-formis*) is a little-known game fish. It is found abundantly in all the lakes of the interior, its range being the same as the lake trout, and extends to the shores of Hudson Strait. It is also found in the rivers, where it frequents foam-covered eddies along with trout and *ouinaniche*. In fishing for these latter I

have frequently hooked whitefish, especially
with rubber-winged May flies or with midges
on No. 12 hooks, as they very seldom take the
larger trout flies. When hooked, the whitefish
is very game, jumping like a landlocked salmon and fighting harder than a trout. As
their mouths are very tender great care is
necessary to successfully land them.

The list of game fish of the peninsula closes
with the pike (*Esox lucius*) and the pickerel
(*Stizostedium vitreum*). The former is found
in all the rivers and most of the lakes northward to latitude 56 degrees; the latter only
occurs in the western rivers of the southern
watershed and in the southern rivers of the
western watershed. The pike ranges from two
to twenty pounds in weight, while the pickerel
are generally taken weighing from four to ten
pounds.

In the foregoing short notes on the game of
the Labrador Peninsula, I have endeavored to
give a brief and as accurate a statement as
possible of the numbers and range of the
various species, in order that it may serve as
a guide to any sportsman who may think of
trying his luck in that region. I have rather
underestimated the chances of obtaining good

sport after any particular game, and have pointed out the difficulties in connection with travel in the interior. Except for barren-ground caribou and bears, only moderate sport can be expected with the rifle; excellent shotgun shooting will be found about the shores of James Bay, and good sport may be obtained in many places along the coast, but in the southern interior little use for a gun will be found during the summer.

The fishing requires no apologies, as it is always good; and, to my mind, anyone making a trip inland must do so with the idea of getting plenty of fish, and only occasional good sport with the gun or rifle.

A. P. Low.

Cherry

I had spent a good many hours one October day on the Snake River plains searching for antelope, and it was well along toward nightfall when "Rubber Boots" and I pulled up before the door at the ranch, and I dismounted, leaving Boots to the care of the packer. The day had been raw and cold, and I hurried into the house and to the great open fire. I was a little blinded by the light at first, and turned all my attention to the fire, only replying to the usual question of "What luck?" addressed me by my companion. I was unaware of the presence of a third person until I heard a strange voice say, evidently in pursuance of a conversation which had been interrupted by my entrance: "For those biggest trout, bait with grasshoppers, shove your raft out from the shore, and when they take, just let 'em take, and sit down on your raft, and you are in for a run around that lake."

Looking in the direction from whence the voice proceeded, I observed for the first time a tall, lank, but powerfully built man, standing with his back toward me. I threw some more wood on the fire, and as it blazed up, and seemingly in acknowledgment of my subdued laughter, a grizzled face was turned toward me, and its owner added, "but, of course, you don't want a very big raft."

This was my first acquaintance with Cherry, an acquaintance which has ripened and become closer with years, and on which I have never ceased to congratulate myself. Whatever I may know of woodcraft and hunting is due largely to his tuition. For many years we have roughed it and smoothed it together; found game and found none; and day in and day out he was the best partner it has ever been my good fortune to meet. He possessed the invaluable faculty of always being around when he was wanted, and was ready for whatever might turn up, from trout fishing to Indian fighting; he had an inexhaustible fund of good humor; was always on the alert, game to the core, and willing to endure any hardship. Cherry was a born sportsman, and a living exposition of the noblest innate rules of the art; but he had his foibles and weaknesses, and of these only I speak. I think his greatest failing was the careless manner in which he handled the truth, often with ludicrous results, not the least humorous feature of which was his own entire oblivion of them.

As a youngster, I imagine Cherry's education had been sadly neglected, and one of his queer conceits was to hide his evident deficiencies in this respect. It was decidedly a case where silence was golden, but he much preferred fighting in the open to ambuscading in that fashion, and was never known to confess his ignorance of any subject under the sun. For instance, one year when we arrived for our annual hunt, we were met at the railroad station by Cherry and the other guides with a pack outfit, and journeyed from there to a small frontier town where our supplies were awaiting us. On reaching our destination, we went directly to the post-office, to inquire for any mail that might have arrived, and Cherry accompanied us. The postmaster gave us our mail, and with it a letter which he had had for some time, the address on which was not clear, and asked us if we could make it out. We were unable to do so, and were about to hand it back, when Cherry said perhaps he could tell something about it. As he could neither read nor write—a fact well known to all of us—we were somewhat surprised at his request; but in nowise abashed at the witticisms which it provoked, Cherry examined the letter very minutely, scrutinizing it carefully from every possible point of view, and finally handed it back to the postmaster with the utmost gravity, remarking that "the devil himself could not read it."

When we reached Cherry's ranch we found that his partner had just returned from a trip to the nearest railroad station above, and had brought back a telegram and letter for Cherry. He as well as Cherry was unable to read, and Cherry brought the telegram to me, asking that I should read it, stating, by way of apology, that he "could read books and letters, but he hadn't got along quite as far as telegrams yet." The letter was typewritten, and this he also asked me to read, remarking that he could read "what had been writ in a good common school hand, but that letter had been writ most awful poor."

One of Cherry's most elaborate essays at fiction was what would be known on the stage as "the story of his life."

This narrative he imparted to me while we

were snowbound in camp together up among
the foothills. The bear signs in our section
had become rather poor, and a snowstorm
affording us a more favorable opportunity, we
started out to take advantage of it. But the
storm proved to be rather more than we had
bargained for, and after two days of travel,
during all of which time it continued to snow,
we made as good a camp as possible, and in
the loneliness and solitude that prevailed during that time Cherry took me into his confidence. Many of his stories derived too much
of their charm from Cherry's picturesque manner of telling to be successfully recounted, and
others were imparted only under the pledge
of secrecy, but sufficient may be here set down
to illustrate his varied career and the resources
of his imagination.

Cherry was about sixty; long, lank, and not
exactly what might be called a handsome
man; and as he sat by the camp fire and re-
lated his veracious narrative, the result was
impressive as well as ludicrous. He had been
born in Texas; was a bit hazy as to the loca-
tion, but, as he put it, "by crossing the Rio
Grande twice, and then going between a butte
and a sand hill, he could strike the old home-

stead in the center every time." But whether
he followed his back track or not, he said, it
would be easy for him to get there when he
struck Texas; everybody down there knew
the place. As a matter of fact, it was on his
father's ranch that old Noah had built the
Ark; it was famous on that account, and
about everybody in the State had been there
at one time or another to look at the place,
and secure a few chips as souvenirs. He recalled the days of his youth, when evil times
came not, and he could travel eighty or ninety
miles a day easily, always on the run, up hill
and down; how, when he was fourteen years
old, he had left his father's house to go to
work on a cattle ranch, and when, after six
months, word came to him that his father's
fortune had been lost in an unlucky specula-
tion, he had returned, and emptied out of his
pockets $80,000 in gold, which had tided his
father over, and saved the family from degra-
dation. He also told me that his name was
not Cherry, but Ryan, and that he had two
brothers, one of whom had become known to
fame as Doc Middleton, the notorious road
agent and confidence man, while the other
had acquired a scarcely less enviable reputa-

tion under the pseudonym of Dick Turpin.
The reason why he had himself assumed an
alias was one of the things imparted to me in
confidence. He had left Texas many years
ago and journeyed to Montana, where he had
started a ranch, and introduced a breed of
horses which he said had since become known
all over the world under the name of the
"Suffolk Punch." Of this stock he had some
80,000 head, besides the ordinary breed of
horses, cattle, sheep, etc.

As fortune smiled upon him, he had "done
society" a little, as he expressed it, and, wishing to marry and settle down, had paid court
to the fair daughter of a neighboring cattle
king. While, from Cherry's account, the attractions of this young lady were not such as
would entitle her to pre-eminence among her
sisters in the capitals of the effete East, they
seemed to have secured for her decided pre-
cedence in her own circle of society, and suit-
ors came from far and near. While Cherry
was far too delicate to go into details, he gave
me to understand that his attentions were not
unfavorably regarded by this damsel, and that
he might long ago have been settled down to
a happy matrimonial existence with the object

of his affections, had it not been for his prospective father-in-law. Why the stern parent objected was not quite clear, but he did so, and finally his animosity attained to such a pitch that Cherry thought it safer to leave the country, as the old gentleman was a dead shot and afflicted with a villainous temper. Being offered the alternative of migrating or of making a target of himself if he remained, he chose the former, and was forced to depart on such short notice that he was compelled to leave behind him his 80,000 Suffolk Punches, his ranch, and everything else of value he possessed. Up to the time of this conversation Cherry had not succeeded in retrieving his fortunes, but lived in the daily hope of doing so, and, indeed, according to his own account, Dame Fortune had so often and so unexpectedly taken a hand in his affairs that I should not be surprised at anything that might happen. I never read an account of some new western Monte Cristo that my thoughts do not instinctively turn to Cherry, as the possible possessor of this hastily acquired wealth. He could travel the whole road from poverty to wealth and back again in less time than any man I ever heard of.

Cherry

The storm having blown over in a couple of days, we broke camp and started for the ranch, and on the way ran across the tracks of an enormous grizzly, and, as luck would have it, caught up with him, and, having a fair shot, I killed him almost where he stood. As we were taking off his hide, Cherry told me about the last one he had killed, and as the story progressed, I began to feel that this one was only a cub in comparison. According to this narrative, while he and his companion had been trapping on the upper waters of the Gros Ventre two years before, their trap had been set and been sprung, but the bear had somehow managed to escape. The same thing happened a second, and then a third time. Exasperated at such unbecoming conduct on the part of the bear, Cherry and his companion resolved that they would have him at any cost, and they set a spring gun by the trap, and also a spear with a dead fall, to pierce the wily animal's back. The next morning they found that the trap had been sprung, the gun had gone off, and the spear lay buried in the ground, but the bear had evidently escaped without a scratch. This was too much for Cherry's companion, who insisted upon taking up the death-dealing apparatus and letting the bear go, but Cherry pleaded for one more trial, and the next morning was at the trap as the sun rose over the hills, to see what had been the result of this last experiment. He found everything just as it had been left the day before. Apparently the bear had either risen later than usual, or had secured his breakfast elsewhere at less personal risk to himself. So Cherry, after examining his rifle, made himself as comfortable as possible behind some bushes, and waited. Morning passed and noon came, and still no bear; but shortly after the sun passed the meridian, there was a crashing among the underbrush, and there came into sight what I judge, from Cherry's account, must have been not a grizzly bear, but one of those antediluvian monsters known as a cave bear, which were the terror of our prehistoric ancestors. Cherry was an old campaigner in bear hunting, and not easily dismayed, but the sight of this tremendous brute as he came leaping toward him, clearing the intervening logs at a single bound, and making the earth tremble at each succeeding jump, was so startling as to make him turn "goose-flesh" all over, so that, as he expressed it, "you could have struck a match" on any part of him. Realizing that discretion was the better part of valor, Cherry, like Brer Rabbit, "laid low," and with bulging eyes watched the bear as he finally landed with one hind foot square in the number six trap. This would have doomed an ordinary bear, but not so this one, and with the most intense astonishment Cherry watched him with the greatest deliberation press down the springs with his front feet, and then open the trap with his disengaged hind foot, and step out, apparently little the worse for his experience.

Up to this time Cherry had been so much interested in the bear's operations that he had forgotten all about his rifle, and it was not until bruin had dodged the spear and started to make off with his booty that he remembered it. He got in two shots on the bear then, but seemingly with no other effect than to put him into an extreme state of irritation, and in this disagreeable mood he started for Cherry on the run. The situation was certainly precarious. Cherry tried another shot, but, as ill-luck would have it, the cartridge missed fire and the ejector refused to work. In the next second or two Cherry thought of

all those things in this world that he should
have done, but had left undone, and of all
those other things which he should not have
done, but had done; but the instinct of
self-preservation was still strong within him.
and an open tree-trunk presenting itself at
this opportune moment. he made a dive for
it. It had been felled to the ground in some
terrific battle of the elements years before. and
Cherry got into it just in time to feel the
bear's claws tickle the soles of his boots, as he
jammed himself into its farther extremity. Do
the best he could, this was as far as the bear
could reach. He was baffled for a moment
only, however, and then Cherry felt his im-
promptu habitation suddenly elevated into the
air and borne along at a rapid rate. Working
himself down to the opening again, he found
that the bear had picked the log up on his
shoulders and was making for a large beaver
pond about three hundred yards distant, from
the steep bank of which he dropped it into the
water, and then sat down to lick his wounds
and await developments. Foreseeing what
was coming, Cherry had taken such precau-
tions as he could to keep his rifle dry, and as
the log floated high enough out of water to

enable him to breathe after the first ducking,
he set to work to remove the obstructing cartridge; but it was slow work, and he labored
under great disadvantages. Meantime the
bear grew impatient, and evidently decided to
force the fighting, for he walked out on the
dam and tore a large section out of it. The
pond drained rapidly, and, to his horror,
Cherry soon felt the impetus of the current
drawing him with ever increasing rapidity into
the clutches of the bear, who was at the opening, balancing himself on three legs preparatory to reaching for his victim with the fourth.
When Cherry reached this point in his narrative I took a good look at him, to see if he
was really present in the flesh, so completely
did he seem to have closed every avenue of
escape. But it seems a new cartridge did go
home finally, and as he made the last cut with
his skinning knife, he told me that that hide
brought him $60 green.

Apparently no adventure ever happened to
Cherry that did not remind him of some parallel instance in which he had figured, usually of
a much more dangerous and exciting character. One year, while we were hunting in an
extremely rough and broken country, we came

across a good-sized bear, and finally, after a
hot chase, brought him to bay on a narrow
trail running around a huge cliff, where we
killed him. His death struggles sent him
over the cliff and to the rocks below. All
of these circumstances brought vividly to
Cherry's mind an adventure which happened
to him some years before, while hunting bear
in the Sierra Madre Mountains. The country
was rough and almost impassable on horseback, and finally he came to such a place that
he was compelled to dismount and seek a way
out on foot. He found a narrow trail with a
high bluff above him and a precipice below,
and had reconnoitered this for some distance
when he saw, rounding the turn ahead of him,
a huge California grizzly. He had left his rifle
behind him, so hastened to make retreat in
good order, but on turning the curve behind
him, he beheld to his horror another grizzly
coming in the opposite direction. For thousands of feet, so it seemed to Cherry, the cliff
rose above him almost perpendicularly, and
the descent into the canon below was just as
steep. Most men in a similar predicament
would have ceased to think of the affairs of
this earth and concentrated their attention on

the next world; but not so the resourceful
Cherry. Short as was the time for deliberation, his fertile instinct was equal to the occasion. With the rapidity of a lightning-change
artist, he proceeded to divest himself of his
clothing, which he tossed over the cliff, and
then, throwing himself on all fours, he proceeded to meet the advancing grizzly. In
those days, as he explained, he was a most
powerful man, and covered with a superabund-
ance of hair. This latter acted as his disguise,
and, putting on a bold front, he awaited the
approaching grizzly, which growled and
showed his teeth as he came up. Cherry did
likewise. They drew closer, and putting their
noses together, both bristled up and growled
louder and fiercer. The bear sniffed at
Cherry, who returned the compliment. The
bear pawed the earth. So did Cherry; and
then, with bristles erect and a parting growl,
each went his way, with an occasional snarl and
a look backward, until the next turn hid them
from view. As Cherry was whittling a stick and
putting some sand on it, preparatory to sharp-
ening his skinning knife for removing the hide
of the bear, he remarked that that was about
as close a call as he had ever had, but, as he

stated with an air of apology, he knew it was all right, "because it was November, and March is the only month that counts for me. I always notice that if I manage to get through March I always live the rest of the year."

While not an admirer of Indian character in general, Cherry paid the "sincerest form of flattery" to one of them in the person of Iago, and at one time this trait of his came near getting all of us into trouble. The last year we were together, the Indians, always more or less dangerous, were especially treacherous. They would get together in small raiding parties, and swoop down on defenseless cattlemen, disappearing as quickly as they came, and leaving a trail of murder and desolation wherever they went, until finally the Government had to send several troops of infantry and cavalry to protect the lives and property of the settlers. One day our party surprised one of these murderous bands and made them all prisoners, and were marching them to the nearest army post, when, at a given signal, they made a break for liberty. Most of them escaped; a few did not. Some time afterward the State authorities sent an agent to inquire into this part of the "massacre," as the "new journalism" styled it in flaming headlines. Knowing he had been in our part of the country, we instructed Cherry to be most discreet, and not to boast, as was his wont, over the Indians he had accounted for. As a matter of fact he had not accounted for any of them.

It was not long after this that a stranger rode up to the ranch, and, following the hospitable custom of the country, Cherry hailed him and invited him in. Some twelve or fifteen of us were sitting outside the door at the time, most of us young fellows, and the agent, as he turned out to be, nodded in our direction, and asked Cherry if those were all his. Cherry took a look at the throng gathered in front of the house, and then turning on the agent, asked him, in a tone of undisguised contempt, "if he took him for an incubator?" He soon got on the good side of Cherry, though, by telling him that he had heard what a good shot he was, but during the dinner that followed, adroitly remarked that he supposed that the Indians whom Cherry had had in charge had escaped. Up to this time Cherry, who had all the time been eager to give a full account of the entire transaction, had managed

to restrain himself, but this slur on his ability
as a marksman was too much, and, in spite of
all our winks and nudges, he came out with an
emphatic, "No, sir; not much, they didn't;
not by a d——d sight." Anything could be
questioned but the accuracy of his faithful
rifle. I do not know what the agent reported,
but am certain he could have had the entire
band of Indians satisfactorily accounted for if
he had remained long enough in Cherry's
society. We took care, however, that he did
not.

It was the year that young Robert Ray
Hamilton was lost that Cherry's pride receiv
ed its quickest fall. The horse that Hamilton
had ridden was found on the bank of the
river not far from our camp, with the saddle
overturned, an antelope strapped on behind
the cantel, and some river grass clinging to
the stirrups. In the hope of finding his body,
we built a log canoe for the purpose of searching the river. Men accustomed to handling a
boat were requested to step out from the mot-
ley crowd gathered on the bank, and among
the first of the volunteers came Cherry, with
the remark that, "he was born and bred in a
boat." We shoved out from the shore, and

began poling along the shallow stream. All went well until we struck a deep and stagnant pool, when Cherry suddenly dropped his pole, and, peering over the side, gasped out : " Boys, we have got to turn back ; I can't see no bottom here." Nor could he be induced to get into an upright position again and go to work until the bottom was once more in plain sight.

One of my most amusing experiences with Cherry happened that same year. Reports of remarkably good shooting had come to us from the other side of the range, and, hoping to participate in it, we decided to cross, although it involved a trip of some 300 miles in the dead of winter. We had almost succeeded in reaching the foothills, when a blizzard from the north struck us with such severity that for four days it drove us before it southward. The country back of us was in such condition, and the cold so intense, that we then decided to strike out for a town about ninety miles distant, to rest up and supply our larder before again venturing into the mountains.

After two days of forced traveling we reached the town, and gave an eager welcome to the first place of entertainment we could find, leaving our horses outside. The latter did not relish this arrangement, and soon became restless, so that Cherry finally decided to take them to the outskirts of town, and make camp, where we were to follow him later. We were just beginning to luxuriate in the comfort and warmth of the hotel, when we were startled by a series of piercing yells and curses almost outside the door, and, recognizing Cherry's voice, we rushed out, vaulted into our saddles, and drove our horses pellmell around the corner. The sight that met our eyes was sufficiently exciting to cause all of us to hurry to the rescue. Our pack horses were bucking about in every direction; some running away; some tangled up in the wire fences, and in danger of serious injury; and some on the ground, thrown by their loosened lash ropes. Cherry was afoot, the bridle of his horse in one hand and his six-shooter in the other. The cause of all this commotion was a trolley car, which had suddenly burst around the corner with the usual clanging of the bell and pyrotechnic emission of sparks. When we arrived on the scene, Cherry had the motorman covered with his revolver, and was bawling to him at the top of his voice to "take his wagon into another street." This

Cherry

order not being obeyed with sufficient alac-
rity, he fired a couple of shots across his bows
as a gentle warning, which confirmed the
motorman and his fares in the impression that
a hold-up was in progress, and the last we saw
of them they were scuttling across lots to a
place of safety. We hastily got our outfit
together, and started at once in the direction
of the old ranch, concluding that, after all,
there was no place like home. Cherry listened patiently to our remonstrances as we
rode away, but was evidently not placated,
and declared defiantly, as the town disappeared behind the hills, that " No Christian
soldiers, with their church-bells ringing, could
travel up the same cañon with *his* pack
horses. Not if he saw 'em first."

It must not for a moment be assumed from
these stories that Cherry was at all deficient
in courage, and nerve, and daring. Far from
it. And while he was not what is known as
a "bad man," and had no private graveyard,
yet many a western bully has found to his
cost that, underlying that childlike and amia-
ble simplicity of character, there was a stratum
as hard as flint, and which struck fire as
readily when dealt a blow. Unless the tradi-

tions of the frontier are at variance with the facts, there are several people registered in the next world on Cherry's introduction. According to one of these stories, Cherry and a number of trappers and cattlemen were gathered at a ranch one winter evening exchanging yarns, as was their wont, and everything was peaceful and amicable enough until the advent of a tough citizen from the foothills, who came in just as Cherry was relating some of his experiences, to which the newcomer took most decided objections. Cherry stood his abuse and ridicule as long as possible, and, finally, when it became unbearable, resolved, rather than have trouble, to leave, and was in the act of mounting his horse when this bully, who was of enormous size and strength, dealt him a terrific blow on the head, which nearly rendered him insensible. He then followed up this cowardly advantage with several more of the same kind, after which he dragged Cherry back to the house and threw him on the floor, as an example of what others might expect who incurred his displeasure. He had made a very grave mistake, however, in giving Cherry this brief breathing spell, for it enabled him to pull himself together and col-

lost his faculties. One of his eyes had been
rendered useless by a blow it had received,
and the other was nearly blinded by the blood
which flowed from a cut on his forehead ; but
as soon as he was able to distinguish his antagonist he made for him with a rush. Seeing him coming, the bully drew his revolver,
but before he could pull the trigger Cherry
was upon him, and before the others could interfere, had they been so disposed, had killed
him with his own weapon.

I happened to be present at a little tragedy
in which Cherry took part, which caused the
death of a famous horsethief and his partner,
and which well illustrated Cherry's coolness
and nerve. He had known years before in
Montana a man by the name of Murphy, who
at that time was acting as foreman for a large
cattle company, and afterward got mixed up
in some one of the numerous border frays
which were continually arising, and the other
side getting the upper hand, he was forced to
leave. While *en route* south he fell in with a
man by the name of Spalding, who had some
two hundred head of horses with him, which,
he assured Murphy, were all "good" stock,
and offered to give him an interest in them if

he would help to get them to market, and this proposition Murphy accepted. Shortly after this they fell in with Cherry, who was returning from a hunting trip, and Spalding made the same proposition to him, which was also accepted. The very next night a band of horse thieves, or sheriff's deputies—they never knew which—stampeded their outfit, and made off south. They succeeded in recovering the greater part of the stock; but, fearing further depredations, and being near Cherry's ranch, decided to winter the stock there.

During the winter a trapper from the north, who stopped over at the ranch for the night, told Cherry that the horses had been stolen, and that Spalding was the man who had done it. Cherry questioned Spalding on the subject, and, much to his and Murphy's surprise, learned that the charge was true. Cherry was for washing his hands of the whole outfit, but Murphy decided to see it out, and, chiefly on his account, our old guide concluded not to interfere, but to allow 'the stock to winter on the ranch and let matters take their course. The winter was almost gone before anything further was heard of the stock; but the latter part of March word came to Cherry that a strong Montana posse was headed for the ranch. Even then he and Murphy took no measures to disassociate themselves from their suspicious company, but decided to stick together, and take chances. Our party was camped on the river, about two miles below the ranch, and one morning in April we heard the posse go by on the gravel bank below, and by the time our horses were caught and saddled, we heard the shooting in the distance. We found out afterward that Spalding had gone to the cow barn about the time the posse arrived, and the leader met him at the door as he came out. He was at once covered with revolvers and ordered to surrender, but, instead, he jumped back into the barn, and opened fire with both his guns. The odds against him, however, were too heavy, and he was shot down where he stood, but not until more than one poor fellow had been sent to his long account. Spalding was riddled with buckshot, and a fusilade of Winchesters was kept up long after he was dead, so that we had to bury him in a blanket.

Murphy, hearing the shooting, grasped his rifle and started for the barn, but just as he opened the door of the ranch, a bullet imbedded itself in the wood near his head, and sent the splinters flying into his eyes. Dazed and blinded for the moment he put his hand to his eyes, and half stepped, half fell back into the doorway, and the man who had fired the shot, thinking he had killed him, raised himself from behind the mound where he was hidden. Quick as a flash, Murphy killed him with his gun at his left shoulder, and almost in the same instant shot through the heart another of the deputies, who incautiously showed himself in another direction. Then he stepped into the open, and called out that he would fight them one at a time, or surrender, but, even while he spoke, a bullet struck him in the back. He turned to face this new foe, but was struck again and again until he reeled and fell, but even then, though shot through in a dozen different places, he continued to use his rifle, and when they got to him the magazine was empty. The posse had surrounded the ranch when we rode up, and commanded the occupants to step forth. Cherry was the only one. As he came out of the door he was ordered to throw up his hands, while forty deputies covered him. He had his hands in his pockets; started to obey the order; drew them half way out; hesitated; shoved them back, and finally crossed his arms on his chest. The order was repeated, but Cherry, looking about him, first at the posse confronting him with levelled rifles still smoking from their recent execution, and then from the body of Spalding to the body of his friend Murphy, both riddled with bullets, he deliberately put his hands back in his pockets, and, turning to the Sheriff, said: "These hands will go up for men, not for murderers."

Cherry will be sixty his next birthday.

Lewis S. Thompson.

An African Shooting Trip

In the fall of 1893, Dr. A. Donaldson Smith, now the well-known African explorer, and I found ourselves in London, with but three days in which to make ready for the African shooting trip we had planned for the following winter. Most of the time during these three days was spent in buying big rifles for ourselves, guns for arming our native followers, tents, provisions, water-filters, water-bottles, and large metal barrels for water transportation. These last proved very useful in crossing the waterless plains. By hard work and rigid economy of time the most necessary things were procured, and on October 13 we were steaming down the Thames in the P. & O. boat Oceana, bound for Aden, in company with an Englishman, H. K., who was to make the expedition with us. The P. &. O. boats carry no explosives, and so, before reaching England, we had been obliged to order cartridges for the heavy rifles we in-

IN CAMP AFTER THE LEOPARD HUNT.

tended purchasing in London sent to our destination along with the other ammunition; we therefore found ourselves in the curious position of being obliged to buy such rifles as would fit our cartridges, a condition of things which greatly amused the gun-makers. Fortunately we found the rifles we needed, and they did us good service.

On the passage out, we added to our stock of provisions and medical supplies at Malta and Port Said. On arriving at Aden we found it the hot and forsaken place it is always pictured; but, labor being very cheap, we easily cultivated the habit of sitting on the pleasant stone veranda of the hotel, while natives moved back and forth between us and the different shops.

We fell in here with anEnglish officer, Captain Swayne, who gave us many valuable hints in regard to what we should carry as food for ourselves and men, and the best method of packing it up for camel transportation. This last is a very important matter, as the boxes or bags must be of a certain size and weight and properly distributed on the camel's back; otherwise, you are sure to have a camel with a sore back in a short time, and in this condition he wastes away and soon becomes useless. Our own provisions were packed in boxes, each holding sufficient to last two weeks. This method proved very efficient as a restraint on the extravagance of our native cooks, as they were told under no conditions would a new box be opened until the time limit of the last had expired. The provisions for our men, consisting mostly of rice, dates and ghee—clarified butter made from camel's milk—were put up in boxes, sacks and tins, respectively, and were easily made into suitable camel packs. There happened to be a boat in the harbor just arrived from the Persian Gulf with a large cargo of fine dates on board, from which we supplied ourselves abundantly.

Finally everything was stowed away on a small steamer, and, after a three days' trip, we arrived, in very rough weather, off a small village on the African coast. The sea was so high that at first it seemed impossible to land; but during the course of the day all our goods were taken safely in, and we, ourselves, carried ashore on the shoulders of natives. It was an anxious time for us, as we sat on the beach watching our gun and cartridge boxes while they were being brought through the surf, as the loss of any of these would have been irreparable. Notwithstanding the fact that the coast abounds in sharks, the natives give no thought to them. They are admirable swimmers, and the water about the dhows swarmed with black heads, all eager to earn a little silver by carrying things ashore.

On landing we were most kindly received by the English resident, the only permanent white man there; and, after a few days of preparation, he sent us off into the jungle, with a caravan of forty-five camels, as many men, and six to eight ponies. We carried with us in our metal barrels some distilled water brought from Aden, as the water on the coast had a bad reputation; well-earned, we thought, when we had pointed out to us, near the resident's dwelling, a small, white stone, upright in the ground, and were told the former resident rested beneath it.

Shortly before we started inland an accident happened to A. D. S.'s camera, which crippled his photographic work a good deal. While taking some photographs one evening, he noticed that the film-roll turned very hard, and finally something broke inside the camera.

We hunted up a dark place in the cellar of the resident's house, and, opening the camera, found the film torn completely across, not having been turned evenly on the supply roll. We took the film off, and, when about to replace it, were uncertain whether the glazed or dull side should face the diaphragm. All were in favor of the glazed side, but on opening both of H. K.'s cameras, we found the glazed side facing front in one and the dull side in the other. H. K. had loaded one of the cameras himself, but had forgotten which one it was. Then both men suggested that I open up my camera to settle the matter. This I positively refused to do, as I knew little about the inside of the machine, and wished to run no risks. The film was finally replaced, and all would have been well had the back of the camera been closed tightly. Unfortunately, a little crack let in sufficient light to damage many of the photographs.

Before leaving the coast, we tried the shooting and kicking qualities of our large rifles— eight-bores and ·577's—experiments for which we had previously had no time. The eight-bores were very accurate, and, considering the 10 drams of powder and 2-ounce ball, shook us up comparatively little. The .577 rifles, with 6 drams of powder and 610 grains of lead, made themselves felt rather more, probably because the bullet was rather heavy for the weight of the gun. The last-named rifles, however, proved very strong hitters. All told, we had about twenty guns, which made it possible for us to go into the best shooting districts, the wandering native tribes, which are very frequently met with, rarely giving trouble, provided you have a good number of firearms. To be sure, we were told of an Italian who got into a little difficulty with the Sultan of one of the interior tribes, and arrived on the coast covered only by his pyjamas, and minus all his outfit; but we soon acquired confidence in our men, and felt uneasy only when all three white men were away from the camp at the same time.

The people on whose coast we had landed are a combination of the Arab and African Galla, and unite the intelligence of the former to the hardy, enduring qualities of the latter. Of medium height, they have, for the most part, well-shaped heads, without the retreating forehead of the blacks, prominent cheek-bones and strong jaws. They are usually lightly built, and with the muscles of the arms and legs rather small and flat; but the chests are well developed, and the pectoral and back muscles invariably stand out finely. The large, flat feet of the African are not infrequently replaced by slender, well-formed feet, with high insteps. As Mohammedans, they eat the meat of no animals which have not had their throats cut, and been properly bled before death. This is not always convenient or easy to do with wild game, and especially with elephants and rhinoceros. In fact, only one rhinoceros was eaten on the trip, which one we managed to bleed properly before he died. Unlike the Mohammedans of some countries, they do not adhere to the rule of eating only animals with cloven hoofs.

One kind of antelope only—the gerenuk—our men refused to eat; for what reason we were unable to make out, unless that it may be they held these animals as somewhat sacred, because they made praying mats from their skins. Birds and fishes are also excluded from their list of foods, apparently on no religious grounds, but "because our fathers did not eat them." The fact that these natives do not eat fish would tend to substantiate the medical theory that fish-eating is a predisposing cause of leprosy. All along this part of the coast no leprosy is apparent, whereas at Lamu, farther south, where fish is a regular article of food with the natives, there is a considerable leper population.

The men's dress consists of a waist-cloth, and sometimes they throw another cloth over their shoulders, and possibly twist a third piece around their heads for a turban. No matter how quickly or casually this is done, their dress, like that of all Eastern peoples, looks as if it were made on them. To protect the feet, they wear a thick, flat, leather sandal, turned up in front, and held on by leathern thongs twisted around one or two toes. These have to be taken off when stalking game, as they are very noisy.

The women, who are not nearly as good-looking as the men, are pretty well covered with cotton cloth, and often wear a string of beads around the neck. The clothes are generally stained a light brown color by using moist clay—a useful idea where one must wear the same clothing several years. They are a light-hearted, childish people, yet have a great deal of pride, and are generally brave

to foolhardiness. Watching them carefully,
one is led to believe that this recklessness of
danger is due more to pride and natural courage than to a religious belief in fate. This
fearlessness is apt to bring one into curious
situations at times, which one would gladly
avoid, as the natives always expect the
"sahibs" to be in for anything that turns up.
We were agreeably surprised at the extremely
decent way in which the women were treated
by the men; and, what is more, the men did
their share of labor.

One is first impressed on starting into the
jungle by the ability of his followers. With
a good head-man, everybody from the head
shikari, or hunter, down to the camel-men,
knows his place in a few days, and rarely
has to be urged to do his share of the work.
The rapidity with which a caravan is got
under way is simply marvelous. Often we
had hardly time, after being awakened in the
morning by the crying of the camels which
were being loaded, to put on our clothes and
drink our coffee before the whole encampment was in motion.

The supply of water is often a most important matter in Africa, and especially so where

we were, in the dry season. Every move was
regulated by the wells; and one realizes how
precious water really is when he sees men
almost fighting for its possession at a water
hole, or, as in one place, where natives built
fires to keep the elephants from coming down
at night and drinking up what little there was.
At one of the wells we passed, where water
was very scarce, we found a few men and
camels belonging to an Englishman, who was
camped far away in a dry district. The
camels were hung about with water-harns or
carriers, and the small detachment had been
sent down to fill them and relieve the camp.

The natives owning the wells at first positively refused to part with any of the precious
fluid. My head man, Adan, here showed his
intimate knowledge of his countrymen. He
talked persuasively and joked with them, while
gently stroking the gray beard of the oldest
inhabitant, and in half an hour had won the
prized permission. Our metal casks, though
rather large and clumsy, kept the water sweet,
and were much more serviceable than the
ordinary wooden barrels, which, when empty
and well baked in the sun, are apt to shrink
and go to pieces.

In the rainy season, when the country is green, and grazing good on the waterless plains, the natives take their large herds of camels perhaps several days from any water holes, and allow them to graze for a week or more without driving them to where they can get a drink. During this time, the natives and their horses drink camel's milk in place of water. It is not a bad substitute, and, after getting used to the slight acid flavor, I used to drink large quantities of it—both fresh and sour. It will not do for tea or coffee, however, as it curdles them. The camels are, no doubt, oftentimes kept from water longer than is good for them. They are a stupid animal, and, when thirsty, do not nose round like a horse, among the water barrels, to make their wants known. They might go two weeks without giving a sign of thirst, unless when in the neighborhood of wells. Although two out of the three compartments into which a camel's stomach is divided are well lined with pouches exclusively for water supply, and can, by action of muscles in the stomach wall, be shut off from the rest of the cavity, notwithstanding the capacity of this reservoir, it is probably best for a camel to have a drink

88

every few days when possible. The falling
off in the animal's general condition, and especially the noticeable decrease in the size of
its fatty hump, which should occupy quarter
the length of the back, calls attention to the
fact that it requires more water.

Our camels would eat any green bush or
tree, but were especially fond of thorn bushes.
The fact that the thorns were two or three
inches long seemed rather to add to their at-
tractiveness. Camels have been given a very
bad reputation as regards temper and general
disposition, but, so far as our limited experience went, they never really offered to bite,
although we constantly walked among them
about camp, at night, when they were lying
down. The camel mats, put on to protect the
animal from his load, and used by the native
tribes as coverings for their huts, made good
blankets for our men, protecting them from
the cold night air of the inland plateau. The
camel is invaluable to the natives, and, with
their flocks of sheep, constitutes almost their
whole wealth. They are not only useful as a
transporting machine, but many are raised for
their meat, the hump and the marrow bones
of the legs being the choice parts.

Sheep meat is also highly prized, and our men preferred it to any antelope we shot. A part of this preference was no doubt due to the fact that sheep cost us something, and they always expected us to give them a good feast of mutton when any big game had fallen during the day.

The camel is often made use of for shikar work. The natives, armed as they are only with bows and spears, cannot approach sufficiently near the antelope to make sure with these weapons. They, therefore, use their best friend, the camel, and by walking along close to the animal's shoulder, gradually edge in near enough to the antelope for a shot with an arrow beneath the camel's neck. The antelope, being accustomed to see camels about, do not fear them. One beautiful head, I remember well, belonging to the large kudu type of antelope, was obtained by a native who employed this method of stalking.

To finish up with the native livestock, I must mention their ponies. These are hardy little beggars, with lots of endurance. My own pet pony, which was a very good representative of the type, had considerable Arab blood in him. Tough and very sure-footed,

he liked nothing so well as a long run after a
wounded antelope. We were told that gray
and white ponies were used in rhinoceros
hunting. The rhinoceros is made angry by a
native riding a white pony directly by his
nose, and the big brute follows savagely, the
attention of his small eyes being held by the
light-colored spectre dancing ahead of him.
The friends of the rider run on either side,
and fill the hide of the rhinoceros with spears
and arrows. Though the natives have to pay
little attention to their horses, as they never
require shoeing in such a country, they are
extremely careless about the most important
part of the animal in the tropics—the back;
and, when selling a pony, try their best to get
their money before unsaddling. Usually, the
saddle cloth has a suspicious red look, and,
beneath it, if there is no open sore, there are
generally several old scars of previous breaking downs. Being Mohammedans, these people will have nothing to do with dogs, and
one never sees dogs except among the Mit-
gans or bushmen, who are of a lower caste.

The quiet, nomadic, pastoral life led by the
natives often grows tiresome, and the different
tribes are constantly raiding one another.

This seemed to be done more for relaxation than for any other reason, and we regretted that we barely missed seeing one or two of these fights.

Once well started, as our camels were in good condition, we usually managed to cover twenty or twenty-five miles a day, except in mountainous regions. The forty-five camels, swinging along at their halting gait in single file, the head-rope of one fastened to the tail of the preceding camel, reached out for two hundred yards or more, and the men scattered all along the line kept up such a noise that we were obliged to range well out on either side to get any shooting. My daily shooting outfit consisted of two shikaris and my syce, who looked after my pony. The shikaris carried the Winchester and .577, and the syce the shotgun and camera. This combination put us in readiness for anything that we might run into.

The first piece of game I shot was a big bustard—with my Winchester, as I did not dare approach nearer than seventy-five yards. This bird, the same as the Arabian bustard, is of a general brownish color with a mottling of white. He walks about in a very thoroughbred manner, flies strong, and is difficult to approach within shotgun distance. We also met with two smaller varieties of bustards, and these, together with wild guinea fowl and doves, often supplied us with meat when large game was scarce.

It was not many days before we fell in with various kinds of antelope, and soon had specimens of about the smallest known variety, the native dik-dik, or Salt's gazelle. These little chaps, standing about sixteen inches at the shoulder, delicately and perfectly shaped, are found in almost all districts where the country is gravelly and rolling. They jump up like hares from beneath a bush, and make a difficult mark when running in the brush. The horns of the male are about three inches long, and are often partially obscured by a brush of stiff hair which grows up from the forehead.

My first piece of real good luck was in getting an oryx. This animal, about the size of a mule, is certainly the most gamy, in looks and actions, of all the antelope tribe in this region. While A. D. S. and I were stalking some aoul antelope, H. K., who was ahead, drove two oryx within one hundred yards, giving me a good side shot. At the report of the Winchester, they ran off at a fast pace, but we made out a splash of color on the light skin behind the shoulder of the animal shot at, and my next shot taking her—for it was a cow—in the buttock, she slowed up, and a bullet through the spine settled the matter. The horns were slender, and of the fair length of thirty-three inches.

One day the men discovered a bunch of about fifteen aoul antelope, which are about the size of a large goat, and have beautiful lyre-shaped horns. These were off on one side, and my shikari and I stalked them around a hill, by which they were feeding. This brought us within a hundred and ten paces, and gave me a quiet shot at the leading buck. The ball not only passed through his shoulders, but, on running up, we found, lying dead about five feet beyond, a doe, killed by the same ball, though we were not aware that another animal was so near. Still another aoul, offering a running shot at fifty yards, gave me a chance I could not resist. This resulted in a broken hip, which enabled me to get her after a short run. We soon gave up trying to get a shot at aoul from a concealed position, as this was seldom successful. The best plan is to walk quietly toward them by a series of gradually approaching zig-zags, when they do not seem to realize your real direction before you are within shot.

Some live bait put out at night to attract lions or leopards was pulled down by hyenas, and I managed to get one of the brutes with a charge of buckshot. It belonged to the spotted variety, of which there are quantities throughout the country, and their evening call was always with us during the trip. They, of course, offer no sport.

We had already reached the inland plateau, which, for the most part, rises abruptly from the maritime plain. This rough and ragged line of demarkation gives rise to some fine mountain scenery. It certainly appealed to us very pleasantly when we were coming out, after a long time spent on the great, level interior plain. It was toward the end of an afternoon, when the mountains appeared suddenly and distinctly before us as we stood on the edge of the plateau, and we realized sharply that a day or two would bring us to the coast, and that our shooting trip would then be over.

At the end of ten days' travel, we were about 3,000 feet above the sea level, and were entering the country of the Gadabursi tribes, well known for their warlike habits. We, therefore, made a free display of our guns, had regular sentries posted at night, and surrounded the encampment with a thorn fence, or zareba, which was useful in warning off animals as well as men.

We had already seen elephant and lion tracks, and as our men showed great eagerness in trying to find the animals themselves, we had not much doubt but that we should soon become acquainted with some of them. One night we heard, and dimly saw, some elephants near a water hole; but it was too dark for shooting, and the next day we were unfortunate in not finding them. A. D. S., however, who followed up some fresh tracks he chanced upon, although unsuccessful, and obliged to halt for the night away from the main camp, had the monotony relieved by a lion, which came suddenly up to the little camp on his way to a water hole. He immediately began to roar with magnificent effect, and stayed in the neighborhood a good part of the night, which explained the drowsiness

WOUNDED HARTEBEEST.

of the party on the following day. It was impossible to get a shot at him.

For a few days after this we were rather quiet. My men and I came on some very good specimens of the gerenuk (Waller's gazelle), the most curious of the antelope we met with, their long, thin necks and sloping quarters giving them much the appearance of a small giraffe. One evening I got a good opportunity at some wart hogs near a water hole, and wounded one in the leg, which we followed up next day.

Before killing him, I wished to get a photograph of the beast in life, and H. K. engaged his attention so well, while I came up with the camera on the opposite side, that the old boar made a quick, determined charge, and H. K. only saved his legs by holding the pig off with the muzzle of his rifle. We had to shoot him without getting a good photograph, as he resented all close approaches with the camera

We first became acquainted with the lion in the following way. A. D. S. had camped several hours in advance of H. K. and myself. That night he lay in wait behind some brush near a stream of water, with a goat tied out as bait. He had fallen asleep, when he was

97

awakened by a tremendous roar, and realized that something was carrying off his goat. Although it was bright moonlight, the animal raised so much dust that he could make out nothing, and, thinking it might be a leopard, he fired at it with a charge of large shot. The animal disappeared, and when next seen was thirty or forty yards away, and undoubtedly a lion, with a companion. A. D. S. had no more good shots that night, but caught occasional glimpses of both animals on a bluff, so close behind his retreat as to make his position decidedly uncomfortable. Early next morning word was sent back to H. K. and myself to hurry on and take part in the sport. Our camps were not yet in motion, and I was up on the hills after kudu. Some of my men came running and shouting after me, and, when we reached the level, my pony was already there in readiness, and the caravan on the move.

Our men were greatly excited, and hurried us on down a rocky ravine at a rapid pace. They ran alongside, carrying the heavy rifles, and keeping pace with the horses. On coming up to the place where A. D. S. was encamped, we immediately set about tracking up the lions. There was a rather respectable little stream of water running through the valley, along the sides of which grew some good-sized trees, and the ground beneath them was well covered with jungle growth. The men went carefully to work, but the earth soon proved too hard for tracking, and we tried a drive of the most likely piece of jungle.

This proved unsuccessful, and, waiting for night, we all three sat out behind live bait, in hopes of a shot. H. K. was the lucky man. The lions came up to his position about midnight, probably attracted by the far-reaching voice of his bait; and he succeeded in killing one outright, and in wounding the other. In the morning we tracked up the wounded animal, and obtained our first sight of a wild lion. H. K. secured a good shot, as we all stood together, about fifty feet away from the lion. which was in plain sight, and finished him. Both were full-grown male animals, but with scanty manes.

Excepting two or three leopards, nothing of importance was added to our bags until about a week later, when we fell in with elephants.

A. D. S. went off in one direction to follow up an elephant rumor, while H. K. and myself were conducted in an opposite direction by an old native, who said he would guide us to a pool where the elephants came every night. We followed old Kimbaro, the guide, to the water, and that very night, about twelve o'clock, were awakened by our men, who said the elephants had come for their nightly drink. Although it was too dark to see anything, we distinctly heard the big beasts about one hundred yards away, moving about in the water, and making low, rumbling noises.

In the morning we took up the track, and, after following it for hours, under a hot sun, came to a native village, by which the elephants had passed. The argyle, or chief of the village, said he would take us to where the elephants would probably rest during the day. He kept his word, and inside of an hour showed us a herd of about twenty. The country was rolling, rough, and stony, which was well for us, but unfortunately it was very open. This made a very close approach—the most important element in elephant shooting—impossible.

The elephants had got an idea into their heads, and were moving slowly along in a compact body as we approached within shooting distance. I tried several shoulder shots, and very soon one large elephant, wounded in several places, stepped out from the herd into the open, where we were, looking decidedly mad. A ball from my eight-bore broke a foreleg high up, and down he went, but was up again immediately. I then tried a head shot with the .577; the hardened bullet, striking just in front of the ear, passed through the brain, and the big fellow went down for good.

Passing by him, my shikari and I ran up on to some low hills in pursuit of the rest of the herd, which had been held up somewhat by one of my men, who circled them on a pony. Coming up with them in quarter of a mile, I soon had two down without much trouble, but the third one took a lot of shooting, and though he did not actually charge, seemed willing to do so any time. Finally, the .577 again found the fatal spot in the head, just as H. K., who had been looking up a wounded animal, arrived on the scene.

Having no more cartridges, I stood behind H. K. while he killed two more, the last, though not a full-grown animal, charging viciously up, within about twenty feet, before he was finally brought down by a forehead shot. On our return to the village the chief sang a song of victory, and there was much rejoicing.

Two days were consumed in cutting out the ivory, and removing and preserving as trophies the skins from the heads and legs of several animals. While taking off the head skin of the large animal first shot, we found the .577 bullet—one-nineteenth part tin—had passed completely through the skull, and remained partially flattened against the skin on the opposite side of the head. We tried the traditional delicacy of elephant foot, roasted twenty-four hours in the ground, after the manner of the late Sir Samuel Baker, from whom H. K. had received personal instruction, and found a little of it acceptable, but it was rather a formidable dish, when a foot measuring four feet around was brought on as an *entrée* course.

Two nights after the elephant shooting, we were awakened about one o'clock by the sentry, who said something was making away with a goat that had been tied out to attract leopards. We could distinctly hear the brush crackling close to the zareba, and picking up our rifles, with nothing on but pyjamas and sandals, started toward the noise, as it was too dark to see more than a few feet ahead.

We were very close, when I was caught up on some thorns, and, fortunately, as it proved, for we were now within a few feet of the animal, which, though invisible, was making far too much commotion for a leopard. Accidentally looking on the ground, I saw by the light of a lantern, carried by the sentry, plenty of fresh elephant tracks, and we willingly gave up the pursuit. Had we walked into the middle of the herd, instead of bringing up the rear, it might not have been amusing.

The next morning natives reported a herd of elephants about one hour away. Pretty well satisfied with what elephant trophies we had, I determined to get some photographs of living elephants. We managed to get very close to the herd, but the thick undergrowth prevented a satisfactory use of the camera, and the results were poor. I was sure they could hear the click of the ratchet as I turned the film roll; and soon, catching our wind, the herd moved off to an open, elevated piece of ground near at hand.

The desire for more shooting now overcame my principles, and my shikari, who was rather disgusted with the photographing part of the morning's work, hurried on to the open plain, where the elephants stood facing us, having halted at the cries of some of my men who had headed them. What appeared near enough for me, did not satisfy my shikari at all, and we kept on toward the herd until even he was willing to stop, and I knew him well enough by this time to be sure that a further advance was out of place. I fired at the biggest one we could pick out of the herd of twelve or more, as they stood head on. Up went their trunks and ears, and trumpeting, they charged us. There was a long stretch to cover before we came to sloping ground, and no bushes or trees; but, separating, to distract the elephants, we managed by hard running, made tiresome by my 16-pound eight-bore, to reach the incline before they came up to us. As they lost sight of us, and could not get our wind, the elephants stopped and filed off rapidly on one side. This enabled me to place another bullet behind the shoulder of the leader of the procession—the same big elephant I had just shot at, and who

THE BIG ELEPHANT.

showed the mark of the first bullet by blood running down his chest in front. The animals now entered the dense thicket where we first found them. There they stood, hot and angry, and reaching their trunks down into their stomachs, drew up large quantities of water, which they blew over their dusty sides.

Some of the natives now told me that the big, wounded elephant had rushed off by himself down the valley, toward the camp. We immediately started in pursuit, and, after a long chase, during which I tried a few unsuccessful long shots, came up with him in broken ground. This allowed us to gain a little elevation in front, and gave me a forehead shot. Down he went, but he was still breathing when we came up. This elephant appeared very old, and had much the best ivory we obtained.

The ivory from this country, besides being smaller, is harder in consistency than that found in the better-watered regions farther south, and for this reason is not so marketable. The most important ivory industry of to-day is that which makes use of it for covering piano and organ keys. By special machinery, sections of the large, soft tusks from the south are converted into gigantic shavings of desirable thicknesses. The knife-blade, starting from the outside, pares around the circumference of the tusk until it reaches its very core. These shavings are then placed in water, and so soft does the structure become, that the strips uncurl themselves. This results in a very easily worked material, and with the loss of hardly any ivory in the process. The hard northern ivory, on the contrary, is very difficult to work, and not at all amenable to similar treatment. Why this difference in size and consistency varies according to the amount of water in a country is not clear, except that elephants in well-watered regions need large and strong digging implements, as they live largely on roots and bulbs, whereas the animals in less moist districts are largely tree feeders, and, not requiring as large tusks, do not develop them.

The next day we came up with A. D. S., and found that he, also, had been fortunate, and had several exciting encounters to relate.

Our provisions were running a little low, so we sent two men and some camels back to the coast for supplies. Natives attacked them on the way down, but were kept off by firing a few shots, and the little band eventually caught up with us again, with a good supply of rice, dates and letters. It was in this country we fell in with the Sultan of all the Gadabursi tribes, and the same who had stripped the Italian, previously mentioned, of all his belongings. We managed to get along amicably with the crafty old chief, who instructed his son to show us game, and made us a present of some sheep. In exchange, we gave him some tobacco and highly-colored cotton clothes, called kylies. The common cotton cloth, of which we carried a large supply, is the money of the interior, and, curiously enough, is made in New England, and is known throughout a large section of East Africa as "Americany." The English claim it to be inferior to some cloth they have tried to introduce on the coast, but, be that as it may, the natives say their fathers used the "Americany," and it is good enough for them.

The old Sultan became rather a nuisance after the novelty of having him about had worn off, as he hung about the camp expecting to be entertained with picture-books, etc. Fortunately, A. D. S. had brought along a music-box to amuse the natives, and by playing this continually we managed finally to drive the old fellow away. The sick people, who came to us to be cured, troubled us not a little here. In an evil moment, H. K. had said that the other two sahibs were medicine men ; and, when this rumor became well circulated, it caused a serious drain on our mustard plasters and compound cathartic pills.

Since leaving the maritime plain, we had been at an altitude of about 4,000 feet—for a few days from 6,000 to 8,000—and remained at about 3,000 feet for the rest of the trip, except during the descent to the coast. This insured us freedom from malarial troubles. How free the air was from germs will be readily seen from the following fact. Our butter, which we had brought out from London, was sealed up in two-pound tin cans. When opened, these cans lasted each one of us about ten days, and during that time the butter melted to a liquid state during each day, and became solid again at night. Notwithstanding this fact, it remained perfectly sweet until used up.

Although disappointed at not finding more signs of lion in the Gadabursi country, we got some splendid antelope shooting, principally

KLIPSPRINGER.

oryx and hartebeest and a few klipspringer. The last-named, a beautiful small mountain antelope, with curious quill-like hairs, is, like the chamois, very fond of peaks and precipices, and so, is difficult to approach.

On coming down from the mountains into the level country, large herds of hartebeest, with scattered bands of oryx and aoul, showed themselves on the plains. Though apparently stupid, the hartebeest did not prove easy victims. Before they were much disturbed, one could approach within about 200 yards in the open, and take one shot; but to be perfectly sure of heart or lungs, with an express .577, at that distance, is not an easy matter, and, unless hit in a vital spot, these animals generally made off in the herd with apparently little discomfort. The Winchester, .45-90-300, though much more accurate than the .577 express, did not prove as effective as one could wish, when used against oryx or hartebeest at long ranges, hard-hit animals escaping with too great frequency. But there are probably very few horned animals that can match these two species for vitality and pluck.

We used to leave camp in the morning, accompanied by a few men and a camel to bring back the meat, and it was not uncommon for us to return at night, the camel loaded down with all he could well carry. We gave away most of the game to some neighboring villagers, who were glad to have such feasts, and showed their gratitude by giving dances before our tents.

One day, while out shooting in this region, a small herd of oryx ran by in single file, 200 yards or more away. I tried the Winchester on each animal as he passed, and, at the third or fourth shot, an oryx, badly wounded in the left hind leg, suddenly wheeled out of line, and came running down to where we were standing. He seemed very much astonished on seeing us, lay down, and allowed us to take a photograph within ten feet without offering to charge, something they are very apt to do when wounded and at close quarters.

We saw a number of ostriches at long distance, and my syce picked up a fresh ostrich egg, which Abdulla, the cook, scrambled for my breakfast next morning. Though a little coarse, it was fair eating; but, like the elephant's foot, its very size, filling as it did the whole frying-pan, destroyed one's appetite.

ORYX.

An African Shooting Trip

As A. D. S. and I wished to make sure of lion and rhinoceros, we decided to cross the Haud, or waterless plain, lying to the southwest, a five days' journey without wells. H. K., not caring to make so extensive a trip, parted from us here, and made his way slowly back to the coast.

One night, before starting on this journey, while smoking together after dinner, A. D. S. and I were startled to see a considerable number of our men range themselves about us in the growing darkness. The interpreter said they refused to cross the waterless plain without increased pay. Taking the lantern from the table, I walked around the circle, and made out the faces of the malcontents for future reference. We decided to make a firm stand once for all, and sent word to the men, after they had dispersed and were gathered about their camp-fires, that they must be ready to march the following day at the old wages, or make their way back to the coast as best they could. The next morning the spirit of dissatisfaction had fled, largely through the efforts of my head man, Adan, who was always staunch, and an excellent manager of his own people.

We filled up everything and everybody with water—men, camels, horses, goats, etc.— and started on the five days' trip across the desert. Here our metal barrels with padlocks came in extremely well, as we knew exactly how much water was on hand all the time, and there was no chance for theft. The allowance per man was one quart of water a day, and the horses got three to four gallons every other day, which quantities, in both cases, proved sufficient.

Even in the middle of the desert we saw a fair number of antelope, principally oryx and aoul, which shows how little they depend on water. I shot one good oryx and some aoul. The oryx, which I had wounded with the .577, as we were returning from an unsuccessful attempt to follow up some lion tracks, ran a little way, stopped among some mimosa trees, and resented every approach on our part by coming on with lowered head. After dodging about some time, I managed to photograph him while he was lying down.

The trail crossing the waterless plain gave a rare opportunity for studying footprints of game, as the carnivorous animals continually use such paths for their nightly

ORYX.

prowls. The hyena's track was seen everywhere; a slovenly print—like the animal himself—with toe-nail points showing in the sand.
Then there were the leopard and cheetah
tracks, differing because the cheetah can only
partially retract his claws. Most noticeable
of all was the lion track. Clearly outlined,
with no nail points showing, and deeply impressed in the sandy soil, it always made one
think of the five or six hundred pounds of
tremendous energy which had passed by, especially when the track was fresh, and the
men following on the hot trail.

Arrived on the other side of the plain, we
found some fair water, and began to hear
news of lion and rhinoceros. The natives
told stories of lions continually jumping into
the native villages over zarebas, oftentimes
eight to ten feet high, and carrying off sheep
and goats, and of one man, who had been
recently killed by a lion, while watching his
flocks on the hills.

At last, one day, when in good rhinoceros
country, luck came my way. For several days
we had been puzzled in following tracks, but
managed one morning, after many hours' hard
work, to come up with two animals in rather

thick cover. There they stood, forty yards away, their ugly noses lifted high in the air, in complete astonishment. At the report of the eight-bore, they started off at a great pace ; but 100 yards was as far as the largest—a cow— could go, the ball having entered her chest and cut some of the large blood vessels.

The smaller animal led us a long chase, and, when twice wounded, charged quick as a flash when only about twenty feet off, in some high grass. He came right in amidst us, and we only avoided being run down by throwing ourselves quickly one side. My men laughed and joked about it ; but, notwithstanding their good nerve, I saw they were not quite so anxious to close in on him again. He gave in, eventually, to a little more lead. A. D. S. also got a couple of rhinoceros, the last one requiring a good deal of shooting. I managed to get up very close to him as he was going through the underbrush, and so caught him with the camera. By quick work, our men cut the throat of this animal before he was dead, and, this becoming known, the natives quickly swarmed around to strip off the hide and meat. The skin of the rhinoceros is much prized for shields, and the

RHINOCEROS.

natives on the coast know how to make them up very well.

This shooting was done in a very dry country, thickly covered with mimosa, and we were obliged to send a good way for water, which the rhinoceros really does not seem to care much about. We became acquainted here with the so-called rhinoceros bird—a small, insignificant bird, with a harsh, piercing cry that immediately arrests attention. He does not, by any means, always take you to rhinoceros; but, if you follow him long enough, he is pretty sure to bring you to game, a honey tree, a camp of hostile natives, or something else equally interesting.

We were told of a place, about a day's march away, where lions abounded; in fact, though it was the only district in that country where there was good green grass for grazing, none of the natives dared take their herds of camels there, as one man, who had recently ventured to do so, lost several camels by lions, and immediately withdrew. On the way to these attractive hunting grounds, A. D. S. shot his first lion—a fine, large one. I was fortunate in getting a leopard at the same place; and the accompanying photograph shows our camp, with the dead leopard, and three small live leopards brought in by natives. These small leopards played about the camp like kittens, and were very sociable and much at home.

Arrived at the green hunting grounds, we found plenty of lion tracks, and the next morning early, I bagged my first lion. We found he had followed up our caravan track during the night, and, coming up to the zareba, within twenty feet of A. D. S.'s tent, was undoubtedly about to jump in, when the sentry shouted at him. He growled, and turning, saw a donkey, which had been staked outside the zareba, and near which I was, lying behind some thorn brush. In one or two bounds the lion had cleared the space, and all was soon over with the poor donkey My stand was only ten feet away, and, as the dust cleared, I saw the lion holding the donkey up, off the ground, by the throat. Aiming at his neck, I fired, and without any other sound than a long sigh, the lion sank down on the ground in a perfectly natural position, the donkey still in his mouth. The ball had smashed the spinal column close to the skull, and killed him instantly. We shot, alto-

A LION WITH A FATAL TASTE FOR DONKEY FLESH.

gether, six lions in this region, of which number four came my way.

The most interesting situation we were placed in at all was with a wounded animal, which our men tried to drive out to us from a patch of brush. Stationed only thirty feet away, on the other side, which meant only one shot in case of a charge, one thought of all the chances. The drive did not succeed, however, in this particular case, and we were finally obliged to go into the brush, where A. D. S. gave the quieting shot. Our men showed the greatest pluck at this time. They crawled in, until they could see the animal, only fifteen feet away, and called to us to follow with the rifles, which we were compelled to do, no matter what we thought of it. Such bravery of the natives, as mentioned above, is common among these people, and several instances are told of shikaris deliberately grasping a lion by the mane, and pulling him off from a white man whom he was mauling.

Another story is told of an English officer, who was caught by a wounded elephant. While the frenzied animal was trampling the white man to death, his shikari, armed only with a spear, rushed in and prodded the beast with his ineffective weapon. The elephant stopped his devilish work for a moment, seized the native by an arm, and threw him away with such force as to tear the arm from the body. This man still lives on the coast— an example of extreme devotion.

The resident wrote me about an amusing incident which happened to another officer, while on a shooting expedition, some months after we had left the country. This Englishman was awakened out of a sound sleep in the middle of the night, and quickly realized that some large animal had firmly closed his jaws on his arm, and was trying to pull him out of bed. He instinctively threw his other arm around the further side of the light cot bed, and the next tug sent everything down in a heap. He knew by this time the animal was a lion, and was much relieved when the beast, becoming rattled, snatched up the pillow instead of the man, and made off with it. The writer added that the officer was not much hurt, but was very indignant.

A little more luck still awaited me in the green grass country, for it was here I fell in with some lesser kudu antelope, an animal of great beauty, and rarely seen. As my shikari and I were walking down through the green belt one morning, a lesser kudu suddenly sprang into view, and gave me a running end on shot about fifty yards off. We saw he was hit, and following quickly through some brush came on another male kudu, which was crossing only thirty yards away, offering an easy running shot. He only went a short distance, with the .577 ball behind his shoulder. A quick run brought us up to the animal first wounded, which was soon brought down. By good fortune, in stumbling upon these beautiful creatures, we had in a few minutes obtained two fine specimens of a rare species.

While camped here, we had company near by in the shape of a large native camel currier or village. The news had spread that two white sahibs had come on the ground for the special purpose of killing off lion; so these people immediately moved in, and said they would remain as long as we stayed, and kept up the good work of extermination.

We were obliged finally, however, to move on from this happiest hunting ground of all. Our stock of provisions was getting low, and every day made it shrink alarmingly. It was not easy to leave a spot where we had had such good sport, and which, besides, was so well fitted for a camping place that we felt quite at home there.

The green belt—one and a half miles long and half a mile wide—is a broken combination of bunches of mimosa and small meadows, and our camp, pitched at one end against a little forest, looked out on a small green field of grass. Our tents being pitched side by side, we took our meals together, and we spent many pleasant hours after dinner, smoking our evening pipes, making plans for the morrow, and listening to the chattering of the men, their forms dimly seen about the camp-fires against the barrier of the zareba, as they discussed their sahibs, their voices mingled with the cries of the camels, sounds which one gets to like, and would give much to hear once more. But move away we must, and a few marches brought us again to the water holes, which supply the country for miles about. Drilled through the solid rock at some earlier period, by means unknown, these wells are about forty feet deep to the water level. A chain of six or eight men is kept busy all day long, as, standing one above the other on small ledges, which occur at in-

HERDS AND FLOCKS AT THE SPRINGS.

tervals on the sides of the wells, incessantly
chanting, they pass the water up, in hol-
lowed out sections of trees, to the troughs.
The troughs are all day long surrounded by
crowds of thirsty camels, sheep and goats,
which may be seen breaking into a run as
they reach the crest of the bluff overlooking
the wells, and begin to hear the splash of the
cool water near at hand.

A day's march from these wells, while separated from A. D. S., I came unexpectedly one
night on a small village, to find that an Abyssinian, armed with a Remington rifle had, single-
handed, compelled the villagers to pay him
a tribute of sheep and goats. The natives
unarmed as they were, could not resist, especially as other Abyssinians were in the neighborhood. As soon as we had located our
camp, this robber came in a very humble way,
kissed my hand, and tried to make matters
smooth by offering presents of sheep, which
he had just stolen. He was told that unless
he had disappeared early next day he would
be taken to the coast, and, although he was
not about in the morning, he undoubtedly
returned shortly after we left. These people
suffer yearly from Abyssinian raids, and, be-

ing so far in the interior, cannot be assisted from the coast.

Not far from this village, my shikari and I fell in with a big kudu, an animal we had been unfortunate in stalking before, and which is the largest antelope of the country. As we were skirting some low hills in thick brush, we were startled by the sudden rush of an animal which sprang up ahead of us, and caught a glimpse of a pair of curved horns disappearing on our left. My shikari shouted to me to run to the right, and as we came out of the brush, a large kudu, with wide spreading horns, appeared racing along on a little hillside eighty yards away. I was too quick with the first barrel, but the second brought him down with a bullet in the spine.

On our next march we came unexpectedly on two leopards, in a small ravine, which at-tracted our attention by their purring. I hesi-tated a second too long, looking at the beauties, and when I did fire, was obliged to shoot through a small bush, and missed. Twice before I lost leopards when they should have been mine. Once, when I tried to exchange guns with my shikari at a critical moment, and again, by attempting a difficult head on

shot with the 577 when I should have tried
my Winchester.

The waterless plain was ahead of us, and, to
help out the rice and dates, I bought a fatted
camel for the men, who enjoyed it hugely,
drying big strips over the fire, so as to preserve it for the journey. The hump, one solid
mass of fat, weighed at least fifty pounds, but
the flesh had for us a strong, unpleasant taste,
and all we could manage were the marrow
bones, which were decidedly good.

Arrived at the coast by an uninterrupted
journey, we parted from our staunch followers—men who might joke and laugh about
the camp-fire in the evening should you be
killed during the day, while fighting it out
with dangerous game, but whom we admired
immensely for their bravery and manliness—
men whom you knew you could trust to stay
with you at all times.

We were most hospitably received by the
resident, and in a few days caught a boat, and
left with our skins and ivory, thorough believ-
ers in the native saying that Mohammed does
not count the days spent in shikar.

Wm. Lord Smith.

Sintamaskin

The early morning of Thursday, the last day of January, was clear and still. The heavy snowstorm of the day before had ceased during the night, leaving a new layer, a foot in depth, upon that which already lay deep over mountain and lake, and piling itself high upon every branch and twig of the dense forest about us. I had awakened at three, still conscious of the effects of yesterday's long tramp, when Peter and I had followed for eight hours the fresh tracks of a herd of seven caribou, far over steep hills, through heavy timber, and in deep, soft snow, only to find that the waning day bade us strike out for camp; for the further route of our game was still to be disentangled from a labyrinth of tracks made where they had stopped to feed. We had eaten our lunch as we marched, delay being a thing to avoid, and fire out of the question on so fresh a trail; and when we reached camp again, just as darkness closed

in, we were a tired and hungry pair. So it
was with difficulty now that I summoned up
resolution to perform the duty of which the
biting cold upon my face and the snapping of
the log walls of our camp apprised me, and
resisted the insidious argument that I really
was not awake. To leave the snug shelter of
warm blankets in order to rake together a few
almost extinct embers, nurse them into a
glow, and pile the stove full of wood is not an
alluring task at such a time; but camp-fire
etiquette, sometimes relaxed in the milder autumn season, must be rigidly adhered to, even
indoors, in these long, frigid winter nights.
Therefore my companion and I had made the
usual agreement that he who woke first should
forthwith replenish the fire, and as his deep
breathing was now proof that nothing was to
be expected of him, I conquered my slothful
disinclination, and a roaring blaze at last re-
warded my efforts. Then I opened the door
upon such a night as only the northern winter
can show.

Silence, absolute and supreme; the rich
purple-black of the sky revealing its immeas-
urable depth, in which hung, clear and round
and at many distances, the myriad stars which

filled it; in the north the great pale arc of the aurora reflected faintly on the white snow lying over the open space of the river in front of us. But the keen air allowed little time for more than a swift glance; then a match lighted showed the mercury at eighteen degrees below zero—not extreme, but cold enough to make blankets desirable; so I got back into them without further delay, and fell asleep.

The next thing I knew, some one else was poking the fire; the room was warm, and the light of day came through the windows. I turned and saw the red "tuque," straight black hair, and copper skin of Peter lit up by the flames as he bent over the stove. Seeing me stir, he remarked that breakfast was nearly ready, and that the morning was "varry cold." Signs of life now appeared in George, my companion, and soon we were at breakfast, with that appetite which surely is not the least boon of a woodland life. Peter was right about the cold. It was nearly eight o'clock now, and the thermometer stood at twenty-seven degrees below zero, but the cloudless sky and perfectly still air were a promise that this would be the best of all days for a winter tramp. The journey we had planned was a rather long one, and offered a considerable variety of snow-shoeing, but we were in good trim for it, and had no fear of rough climbing or tangled windfalls.

The use of snow-shoes is not a difficult matter, even for the beginner. Like every other form of athletic pursuit, it requires some practice to overcome the awkwardness of first attempts, and to acquire familiarity in dealing with the little complications of woodland travel, such as windfalls, thick bush, and steep places. But the same is true to some extent of all walking, and there is no reason why any one who likes wholesome exercise, and can ride a horse or a bicycle, row a boat or paddle a canoe, should hesitate about making a winter hunt through fear of the much exaggerated difficulties of snow-shoeing.

The first time that I ever put on snow-shoes I started out with the usual stiff-legged, straddling gait of the beginner, and his conviction that the huge and cumbersome things were skillfully designed to impede my progress. The first advice of my Indian instructor was to "limber up" my joints, and walk as though I had no snow-shoes on. Acting upon this, I managed to go a mile up a steep hillside and back again, with tolerable success. The next day I hunted caribou, walking about ten miles. After that we did from fifteen to twenty miles every day, in a very rough country, and in snow that was both deep and soft, my companion being a man who not only had not worn snow-shoes, but had never even been in the woods.

The shoes should be large, and not too heavy; the webbing of the best, and tightly strung. The strings should be of moose-hide, in the aboriginal fashion—the white man's "improvement," of straps, is a snare and a deception. The strings must be carefully adjusted, which takes a little trouble at the outset, but is of the first importance. If too tight they hurt the foot; if too loose they allow it to slip forward, and catch under the toe bar in a way that is dangerous when going down hill. The foot-gear varies somewhat with individual preference; but there should be several pairs of thick woolen stockings or socks, and over these moccasins or felt boots. For one whose feet are not toughened by much snow-shoeing, I advise the use over all of snow-shoe rubbers—heavy rubber over-

shoes without heels. They are a valuable
protection against the chafing of the strings,
which must be worn pretty tight over the
toes, and, by retaining the heat of the foot,
they largely prevent the melting of the snow
under the instep, and its caking on the webbing. They must always be longer than the
foot, to allow ample room beyond the ends
of the toes. With proper foot-gear, then,
good shoes, and a little instruction from an
expert, the beginner may rapidly qualify himself for one of the most exhilarating methods
of pursuing the moose or caribou. He will
not attempt too much at first, and he will take
in good temper, I trust, the little mishaps that
come to him ; and bear in mind that, though
an occasional wild plunge head-foremost into
winter's mantle is alarming, and the subse-
quent struggles rather exasperating, still no
harm results. As for distances, they vary, of
course, with the strength and skill of the individual, the nature of the country, the weather,
and the depth and quality of the snow. I
know men, Indians and trappers, who have
made great distances in a continuous journey.
My own trips to the wilderness have usually
been made at times when I stood in need of

physical recuperation; so that I have not been in condition to undertake great efforts. My best day's tramp was about twenty-five miles. Of course I am speaking, be it understood, of the season of the year when it is still legal to kill game, during which time the snow is soft, except when packed by the wind upon the open surface of lakes. Of the barbarous and unsportsmanlike practice of "crusting" I know nothing by experience.

I write this because I have so often been asked by my fellow-sportsmen whether the art of snow-shoeing were not so difficult as to stand in the way of a winter camping-trip. I think this idea arises partly from the fact that some writers have mistaken their own lack of skill, or want of competent instruction, or perhaps their pig-headedness, for an inherent difficulty in the sport they describe; and I think I have even detected occasional traces of a desire to magnify their own exploits by exaggerating the difficulty of what they have done; but these exaggerations are to be deplored when they tend to discourage others from wholesome enjoyments. But to return to our day's journey.

This was the last day of the open season;

to-morrow the law would stand between our
rifles and the game—no obstacle, perhaps,
save to a sportsman's conscience. George
was safe from a blank score—he had killed
his caribou, a young bull, two days before;
but I had not yet had a shot. Peter had
urged upon me strongly the desirability of our
taking up again the tracks of yesterday where
we had left them, back in the mountains, saying: "Ah 'll t'ought he's not go varry far;
sure he's got wan varry large caribou; that's
good chance for find 'um;" and had this not
been our last day, I should probably have
adopted this plan. But the trip decided upon
was to a point which I had long wished to
reach, and it had been postponed from day to
day since our arrival here, for various reasons.
It offered, moreover, a fair probability of seeing game—caribou, that is, for we had found
no sign of moose upon any of the hills, which
we had explored in many directions. So
Peter's views did not prevail.

Now, as for the place we were going to, I
knew little more than that, some years before,
when poring over a map of this region, lost in
speculations concerning the distant lakes and
rivers, my fancy had been captivated by a name,

the name of a lake—Sintamaskin *—which lay some distance beyond the farthest point I had then reached in my brief camping-trips. Names are misleading. This is a country of many lakes, greatly diverse in character and of very varying degrees of beauty; and I had no reason to suppose that this lake possessed any special charm to distinguish it from the hundreds of others about it. Yet the name lingered in my memory, and in those sudden waves of longing that come to all of us who love the woods, it would recur to me with a strange wild flavor of the far-away northern forest. Gradually, however, it faded from my recollection, and had not been recalled to me until a few days ago, when, as we were setting out upon our trip, a friend, familiar with all this region, said: "You'd better go over to Lac Sintamaskin;" and, after describing it, he added: "You'll see fine timber there; you know it has never had a dam on it." Just what this meant can best be realized by those to whom our northeastern wilderness is known.

* Sintamaskin : the first syllable nasal, like the French *saint ;* accent on the last syllable, which is pronounced as English *kin.* The Algonquin word is *Sattamoshké,* and is said to signify "Shallow River."

Sintamaskin

The first act of the devastating lumberman,
about to ply his trade on any lake and its
tributaries, is to build across the outlet of that
lake a big dam, which, through the indiffer-
ence of improvident legislatures, he is allowed
to leave, and which remains, for years after
his operations are concluded, a hideous monu-
ment to the brutality of man. By means of
the dam the water of the lake is raised far
above its natural level; the shores are
drowned, and their original beauty is forever
destroyed. The waters recede, but they leave
behind them a ghastly fringe of bare stones
and dead gray trees, to take the place of the
banks carpeted to the water's edge with vel-
vety many-hued mosses; the lovely grass-
grown beaches of pebbles and white sand;
the graceful boughs of the innumerable forest
trees which hung over all and mirrored their
shimmering foliage in the tranquil waters.
Sometimes, indeed, it happens, as in the case
of one exquisite jewel of the wilderness I
have in mind—the Little Wayagamac—that a
lake has an outlet which for some reason cannot be dammed, but which furnishes enough
water without a dam to float away the logs on
the spring freshets. In these cases the heavy

hand of the impious and wasteful lumberman
falls less cruelly, and if fire does not follow in
his train, destroying all, we dismiss him from
our thoughts, with curses upon him only for
having cut down all the pines. But Sintamaskin, I learned, falls within neither of these
categories. High upon the very summit of
the hills, and distant only some three miles
from the main river, it discharges its waters
down the steep mountains in a tumbling,
rock-strewn flood, and dam or no dam, the
lumberman cannot handle his logs in that
precipitous descent. Some day he will find
another way, perhaps; but, for the present,
nature's defense holds good, and this spot is
still inviolate. So it seemed that I might
look for some sort of confirmation of my
fancies concerning it. To be sure, now that
the deep snow had blotted out all but the
boldest shore-lines, we could hardly hope to
realize one of the greatest beauties of this still
unmolested lake. But my resolve to go there
was none the less firm, and even George, to
whom the whole country was a new wonder,
caught something of the infection, so that
now both our voices were raised against the
proposal of the Indian to take up again the

trail of yesterday, and our start was made upon the road to Sintamaskin.

For the first time since our arrival in camp we set forth all together, George and I and our two Indians, whom, since they were both named Pierre, we distinguished by calling one Peter and the other Pierre Joseph. They were both typical members of the Abenaki race. Pierre Joseph, whom we found here, is a somewhat morose and taciturn creature, given, say those who know him, to fits of impracticable sullenness at times, which make him an undesirable partner. Hence he tends his traps alone, which are scattered through the woods to the west and north of us, on the upper branches of the Wastaneau and the waters flowing into the Vermillon; and in this vast waste he leads his solitary life, unsolicitous of human companionship, making day by day the round of his traps, with the leathern strap across his forehead by which he drags the toboggan carrying his furs and his supplies. At the end of the day's journey he finds shelter in one of the little round-topped bark wigwams that he has built in convenient places. He is universally conceded to be a skilled hunter, and, despite his rather gloomy reputation, he was always obliging enough while with us.

Peter is a character, an old friend of mine, a tall man of quiet movements. His complexion is somewhat ruddier than is usual among his degenerate people, and his features have something of the aquiline which typifies the Indian. His expression is of both dignity and sweetness, his courtesy unfailing, and his industry untiring. He has the keenest sense of humor, and is a most entertaining story-teller; his voice soft and musical. Altogether he has a winning personality, whose only fault is the old one that has been the ruin of his race, and that has led him into serious trouble more than once upon his return to the haunts of men. And yet so ingratiating is this personality that time and again, by sheer virtue of that alone, he has restored himself to favor among those who had every reason to exhibit only severity. He is a descendant and bears the surname of that captive from the neighborhood of Deerfield, Samuel Gill, whose story Parkman tells in "A Half-Century of Conflict." Now, after nearly two centuries, here was I, in part the descendant of that nation which, through the ferocity of its bloodthirsty savage allies, had been so bitterly hated and so desperately feared by the struggling colonies, and with me as guide in the trackless Canadian wilds was this child of the wilderness, this descendant of the little Massachusetts Puritan.

The first three miles of our journey were northward down the river upon which our camp faced, the south branch of Wastaneau. At this point, about a mile below the lake of the same name, it is a quiet, winding stream, flowing between banks that in summer are low and grassy, with the hills rising behind them on either hand; but now the snow had in great part obliterated the distinction between river and bank, and we cut off many turns of the stream, passing over land where a few isolated twigs, sticking at random from the white surface, were all that indicated the thick bushes I should see when paddling my canoe here the following September. Gradually the hills approached the river and the low banks disappeared; one or two rocks showed their heads in a narrow place. The men went slowly, sounding with poles through the snow to see if the ice were good—the first premonition of what lay but a little way beyond; for

there the river leaped suddenly over the brink
of a ragged wall of rock, and turning sharp to
the east, went dashing and roaring down into
a deep gorge, through which it swirled in
foaming whirlpools and cascades. Cliffs and
great walls of forest-clad mountain rose sheer
above it; between them we saw it far beneath
us, to where it turned around the shoulder of
a mountain and ran off again to the north, to
its junction with the other branches, the
Rivière du Milieu and the Rivière du Nord.
Thence the three streams, united, flow eastward into the St. Maurice—Madoba-lod'ni-
tukw, the Abenaki call it—some twenty-five
miles below La Tuque, ancient gathering-
place of the dreaded Iroquois in their bloody
raids upon their northern neighbors.

At the falls we left the river and began our
climb up the mountain. It was a long and
toilsome ascent, guided only by the blazed
trees—for there was no other sign of portage—and as steep as it is practicable to climb
on snow-shoes. We pulled ourselves up by
branches and the trunks of trees, often holding to them with one hand, and reaching back
with the other to grasp the extended rifle of
the man below and haul him up; continually

fearful lest the soft snow might slide with us bodily, and send us rolling helpless downward. We were up at last, however; and now our path was easier, though still rough, and along the side of steep slopes, and up and down many sharp pitches. We were passing through a heavy forest, our course to the east, about parallel with the ravine of the river. We went, of course, in single file, the men taking turns at leading, for the work of him who "breaks track" is much the hardest. The snow was about four feet deep on a level, and far more than that in places. It was soft, and though our snow-shoes were large—very different from the slender toys one sees in the shop windows of Montreal—our tracks were at least a foot in depth. This meant heavy going for us, though it did not seem to impede the caribou. The trees on our left opened, and our path led near the edge of the ravine. It was just at the point where it turned to the north, and through the snow-laden branches we caught glimpses of a marvelous distance: long walls of mountain, russet and gray with the naked limbs of great hard-wood trees, or deep green with tier upon tier of spruce and fir; here and there the light green of a pine—all hoary with snow lying high upon every branch, even to the very top of the tallest trees; then farther lines of hills, their banks of evergreens showing an unimaginable deep blue in this intensely clear air; beyond all, in the extreme distance, faint, translucent hills of blue and violet melting into the sky, and one clear note of rosy white, a far-away burned mountain.

Next we plunged into dense forest of deep green : the ground was level; were it summer we should be walking on spongy green moss. All about us the tall straight stems of spruce and fir rose high into the air, their dark branches interlacing overhead. Among their feet were the little balsams, an endless wealth of Christmas trees; but here their fragrant branches were adorned only with snow, piled upon them so deep that they were pyramids of white, merely flecked here and there with a green which, by contrast, looked black and colorless. So thick they stood that we could see for only a few yards, and their branches brushed our faces and sent heavy showers and lumps of snow upon us as we passed. The hoarse croak of a raven overhead brought to my mind visions of Norse gods flying through the winter sky — skin-clad and with black wings upon their heads.

Then the ground lifted again, the birches and moosewood reappeared, the forest was more open and more varied, the ground rough and broken. And so, now on rocky hardwood ridges, again through sombre swamps of evergreens, went our way, nearly three miles in all, until at last a sudden downward slope brought us to the border of a little lake. We crossed first this, and next a narrow strip of spruce-grown land, and we had reached Lac Clair.

This is a large, open lake, with fine woods about it, and some picturesque low cliffs along its eastern shore, but not on the whole a very interesting spot. We crossed it in a north-easterly direction, two miles, carefully scanning its unbroken white stretch for signs of game. We found nothing but the record of a little woodland tragedy : the footprints of a hare bound across the lake, at first near together, then suddenly far apart as he had leaped for his life ; approaching, at an angle, other tracks, those of a marten ; then the two mingled, a disturbed place in the snow, drops of blood ; and last, the tracks of the marten back to the shore, partly obliterated by the wide trail of the object he had dragged along.

Off the lake and another climb, stiff as the first, but shorter, three-quarters of a mile through heavy forest, and then Lac Long, head of the waters we had followed. As its name implies, it is a long and narrow lake, through which we passed, and here we saw tracks of caribou—made before yesterday's snow, however, so that they were not of great interest to us. Another short stretch of woodland, and we came to Lac aux Truites. This was Sintamaskin water, and here for the first time we saw the pine in any quantity. Opposite us, about half a mile away, the eastern shore rose abruptly in a bold cliff, and upon its brow and on every ledge and projection of its face the pines stood in rows, their green plumes clear and beautiful against the blue of a cloudless sky. The cliff extended to the north, past the lake, and formed one wall of a ravine through which the outlet flowed; down this we went toward the object of our journey, a mile away—down a short way, then along a level stretch. The forest was heavy—here and there a big pine, many tall spruces, and massive, splendid gray birches, whose rough bark, always full of color, was now, against the snow, of intense vividness of rose and violet. Then the last slope downward, rough and rocky, and here stood the trees which are, to my mind, perhaps the greatest glory of Sintamaskin—white birches. Not the slender saplings of our local woods, but magnificent great fellows, two feet in diameter, their wonderful bark curling in scrolls where, in its exuberance, it had peeled away; silvery white in summer—or now against the blue sky; by contrast with the snow, they were salmon and golden, their color intensified by the lumps of snow piled up on every projecting edge of bark They grew even to the shore, where they mingled with the cedars, whose feathery branches overhang the clear green water in summer-time, but whose lower limbs were now buried beneath the sloping snow.

We came out upon a long and narrow bay, the southwestern corner of the lake. On the left was a ridge covered with spruce and hard wood; on the right a high and precipitous wall of cliff and tumbled masses of granite, upon which rose ranks of the sombre-hued and rigid spruce and fir, and high above all the graceful forms and lighter green of the pines.

In single file we advanced—Pierre ahead, then I, George next, and Peter bringing up the rear—and as we neared the mouth of the bay the great expanse of white opened .before us ; we saw that its farther shores were thickly wooded and the hills not very high to the east, for the lake lies well up at their tops. In front of us was an island, five hundred yards away ; to the north, others. They were rocky, fringed with cedar, and above these, again, were the birch and pine.

Further examination of the scenery was cut short; for as we reached the open and turned northward along the western shore, Pierre Joseph and I, who were somewhat ahead of the others, saw what brought us to a halt, namely, fresh tracks. They led across our path straight for the nearest island. The caribou were not long gone, and we instinctively lowered our voices to a whisper as we discussed the probability of their being behind the island. But no ; as I looked ahead again I saw another line across the snow. We advanced ; these tracks led back from the island to the shore, and were so fresh that at the bottom of each deep hoof-print the water which overlay the ice under the heavy snow was not yet frozen—a significant fact with the temperature still well below the zero point. There was no whispering now; we raised our eyes to the shore, which was in shade and fringed with a dense growth of cedars. Too bad—they had gone up into the woods; it was past midday, and too late to follow them far; if we had only got here a little sooner!

But hold on! What's that? In the gloom of the dark cedars I saw a dim gray shape, motionless; then another. And now I realized that I had done a foolish thing, one that some years of experience should have taught me to avoid: I had left the cover on my rifle. Slowly and cautiously I drew it off, not daring to make a sudden movement, but breathless with the fear that the game might start; for one jump into the bush and the only chance would be gone. My heart was beating so that I wondered if the caribou would not hear it, when just as I got the rifle free they started—not two of them, but three, and not into the woods, but straight across us out over the lake, about a hundred yards away. They were running, and with a swiftness that demanded quick shooting, and that was surprising in snow which, though less deep here than

145

in the timber, still was such that a man would be practically helpless in it without snow-shoes. They sank so deep that as they ploughed ahead the movement of their legs could hardly be seen, but was more than suggested by the flying lumps and clouds of snow that rose about them. Their thick-set bodies loomed large and dark against the dazzling surface beyond them, and contrasted sharply with their long hoary manes. I sighted on the leader and fired, and as I saw him stagger perceptibly I heard another shot. George had come up and was beside me, opening fire on the second. I kept on at the first one, shooting as long as he moved; but at the third shot he pitched forward and lay in the snow. Then as I turned my head I saw George's beast sinking, and we both fired almost together at the third, now a good long shot, but after another volley down he went, too. Luck, pure and simple, after all; but then we had expended considerable skill during the past week with little to show for it, and this we considered our fairly earned reward. Then we made the tour of our quarry—three bulls. No *coup de grâce* was needed; they were stone-dead. They lay

upon their sides, with heads outstretched, and
the tumbled snow covering up their heavy
powerful legs and big round black hoofs,
which carry them abroad when all other deer
are fast bound by impassable barriers of
snow. Their sleek sides glistened in the sun-
shine, and we saw the color of their bodies —a
hue the exactest balance between brown and
gray; an absolute neutral, which, with their
white heads and long-haired gray throats,
makes them seem of the very essence of the
northern forest and the winter rime.

Our guides began at once to busy themselves with the preparations for luncheon,
always to me one of the most interesting
episodes of a winter day's journey. The foot
of a bold rock on the shore was selected as a
suitable place against which to build the fire;
the snow about it tramped down to make it
more firm. The men drew little axes, shaped
like tomahawks, from the sashes wound about
their waists : one of them attacked a dry dead
tree which stood near by, his unerring strokes
ringing clear and sharp on the still air; the
other vanished within the woods, where he
selected a fir-balsam and cut it down. We
heard the crashing as it fell, and saw a cloud

of snow-dust rise among the trees. Presently he reappeared, bearing upon his shoulder a length of the trunk, which he threw upon the snow before the rock; then away again, to return with a great load of thick green branches, which he piled upon the log. This was to be our seat. Then he turned to help his comrade, who was chopping up the dry wood of the dead tree. They brought loads of this; it was built up against the rock; strips of fat bark were torn from a birch and thrust under and among the sticks, the match was applied, and in a moment the crackling flames were shedding a heat more than grateful to him who, warm and a little tired with the toil of long and heavy tramping, soon had begun to chill under inaction in the keen cold. Meanwhile, one of our Indians had taken the tin pail and gone out a way upon the lake. He took off one of his snow-shoes, and used it as a spade to dig a hole in the snow; at the bottom he found slush, through which he broke with a few blows of the head of his axe. Below again was water, a few inches deep, and under that the ice. He dipped his pail full and returned to the fire. A green pole was driven into the snow, and from the end of it the pail of water was hung over the flames. This was to make the tea, universal comfort and mainstay of the sojourner in the wilderness. The tin cups and plates were spread upon the green boughs; a plate of cold bacon and pork was set near the fire to warm; a loaf of bread was cut into generous slices, which were toasted at the flames upon the ends of sharpened sticks; and in an incredibly short time since it was beginning to seem that this was a pretty bleak place after all, we were basking in the warmth of a roaring fire, and partaking heartily of hot drink and smoking food. Then pipes, lit with hot coals, were never better, and at last we rose, strengthened and refreshed, ready to set out upon the long tramp home, more than ten miles away. It would be long past nightfall before we reached it; but the hills on our homeward trail sloped downward, the moon would be high in a cloudless heaven, and though weary we should be happy: so the rapidly lengthening shadows gave us no uneasiness as we turned our faces away from Sintamaskin.

When next I came it was in the blue and golden haze of a sunny September afternoon.

We had toiled slowly up the long portage
from the St. Maurice, three miles of continuous steep ascent, the men and I heavily laden;
we had reached the lake, and the men had
returned for another load. I agreed to meet
them at the portage on the farther shore, and
then we two, my wife and I, embarked in a
tiny birch canoe. We were in a little landlocked bay, so closed at the farther end by
narrows as to seem a pond; beyond them it
opened out again, and again narrows appeared beyond; thence we passed by deep
winding channels among many islands which
border the eastern shore. The water was
crystal-clear and green; the rocks were mot-
tled with lichens and carpeted with velvet
moss, emerald-green, white, and crimson; the
cedars curved their aromatic boughs over the
limpid depths; against their deep green the
scarlet berries of the mountain-ash blazed in
the sun, and among them stood the silvery
stems of giant birches, their exquisite tops
shimmering green and gold against the blue
of the sky. And above all, upon every little
island and over all the hills, rose the stately
pines, in whose topmost branches the soft
west wind sang the song it sings to all upon

Sintamaskin

whom the wilderness has laid its spell, calling upon us to return again, with a voice that can never be long denied.

To many this is a fine, large lake, well wooded, but in which unfortunately there are no fish ; to a few of us Sintamaskin is a fairy-land.

C. Grant La Farge.

Wolves and Wolf Nature

The dog is usually regarded as the most intelligent of quadrupeds. Perhaps we think him so because we see more of him than we do of any other domestic animal, and perhaps a part of his intelligence is derived from his long association with man; but at all events it is very great by comparison with that of the other animals which we know.

Wolves are only wild dogs, and their intelligence should be of a high order. That it is so, all who have had much opportunity for observation are agreed. The Indian recognizes the wolf as the embodiment of craft and smartness, as is shown by the name for scout in the Indian sign language. He also regards the wolf as a friend, and among some tribes there are people who claim to understand the language of the wolves, and to hold communication with them, receiving friendly warning of the approach of danger. From the hilltop, the wolf barks at the Indian hunter as he passes along, and the hunter calls back a cheery greeting in his own tongue. The white hunter acknowledges the wolf's intelligence, and is divided between his admiration for it and his hatred of the animal for the harm it does.

As a rule the gray wolf is regarded as less intelligent than the little coyote, whose smartness, however, almost makes up for his lack of size.

In discussing wild animals, we are all very much disposed to consider the species as a whole, and to deal in general terms, jumping to the conclusion that all the individuals of a kind are exactly alike, and not taking into account the marked variation between different individuals, for we consider only their physical aspect. We forget that to each individual of the species there is a psychological side; that these animals have intelligence, reason, mind, and that at different times they are governed by varying motives and emotions, which differ in degree only from those which influence us.

Yet if we stop and think, we realize that important physical differences exist between individuals within the same species; that some are stronger, swifter, more enduring than others. If, then, their physical qualities vary, as we know they do, it is only logical to conclude that mental differences may also exist between different individuals. Concerning these mental differences we are much in the dark, yet in the horses that we ride and in the dogs that we have for our companions, we recognize such individuality. If this exists among domestic animals, we may be certain that it does so among the wild ones.

We may feel sure that on them, as on all other animals, two principal motives—the desire for food and the desire to escape from their enemies—act at all times; but besides these, they have other impulses of which we scarcely ever think. As one of these, the hunter recognizes curiosity, which he constantly observes, and which frequently proves fatal, even to those animals which are the most wary and the best able to take care of themselves. Playfulness is always manifested by the young, and often even by old mammals, and is shown also in the habit common to many a carnivorous animal, which disables its prey, and then lets it run off, well knowing that it can easily catch it again; or in the case where a coyote teases a badger to the point of fury, just as a small boy may tease his smaller fellows until they roar with rage. The sexual motive is overpowering at certain seasons. Pride and revenge and grief no doubt are felt. Love of approbation, which is well known to exist in domestic animals, no doubt does so also in the wild. Self-sacrifice is practiced by the mother, who starves that her young may feed. In fact, it is altogether probable that the higher wild animals are influenced by a vast number of just those motives which influence savage man.

Familiar as this subject should be to all, it is yet one about which we think too little. Among the many essays which have been written about it, none is more interesting or more to the point than that given by Darwin in chapters III. and IV. of the "Descent of Man."

One of the strongest evidences of the intelligence of wolves is seen in the fact that they, perhaps alone of all wild animals, at certain times so far surrender their own individuality as to combine to help each other for the common good. The mere fact that wolves hunt in packs is not in itself evidence of the power of organization, but that they hunt together by relays, one relieving another, does show an ability to correlate cause and effect, which comes surprisingly near to what we are accustomed to call human intelligence. I believe that this organizing faculty is occasionally seen in the gray wolf, and constantly in the coyote.

THE GRAY WOLF

The range of the large wolf of America extended east and west from ocean to ocean, and from the farthest barren grounds of the Arctic circle south to the *tierra caliente* of Mexico. Whether the American wolf known as big, gray, timber, buffalo, lobo, or loafer wolf is the same with the wolf of northern Europe, and whether or not the big wolf of America to-day is to be divided into subspecies, is a question on which I believe the naturalists are not altogether agreed. But for the purpose of this article, the large wolf may be considered as one species wherever it is found in America.

Over the greater portion of its range this wolf is gray in color, but in the Arctic regions, and occasionally in the Northwest, it is white or nearly so, while in Florida and some of the

Gulf States, and in British Columbia, it is black. In Texas there are red or bay wolves. The hair of the black wolves which I have seen from British Columbia was not wholly black, though the color of the hide was so. By parting the fur it could be seen that near the skin the hair was dark gray, and that only the tips were black. In the same way, many of the gray wolves of the West have the under coat pure white, but the long hairs being black tipped the whole effect is gray.

More or less difference in habit, caused by conditions of its environment, is found in this species. The wolves of the North live to a considerable extent on reindeer and caribou; those of the East on deer, while those of the South prey largely on deer and on the wild hogs which run at large through the pine forests and swamps. Years ago, the center of abundance of the gray wolf in America corresponded very closely with the centre of abundance of the buffalo. Great numbers of these always hungry animals accompanied the buffalo herds, killing calves or old bulls, and sometimes cutting out from the herd strong young heifers, which they had little difficulty in pulling down if once they could separate them from the companionship of their fellows.

In the eastern United States the wolf is almost extinct, but in the unsettled parts of Canada it is still to be found in considerable abundance. In 1893, and again in 1895, wolves were killed in the Adirondacks, but I know of no authenticated recent capture of this species in Maine. In 1895 a litter of wolf cubs was reported to have been killed not far from Jerseyville, Ill., the mother having been seen in that neighborhood several times in previous years. In the Southern States, in sparsely settled districts near the Gulf of Mexico, wolves are said to be even now not very uncommon, and within a few years past several have been seen in the wilder and more mountainous portions of Tennessee.

It is not until the Missouri River is crossed, however, that the wolf occurs in any abundance; but when the cattle country is reached they are found to be more or less numerous, though they do not increase nearly so fast as does the coyote. At the same time in many sections of Montana, Wyoming, Colorado and Texas, they are numerous enough to cause very serious loss to the stockmen.

Notwithstanding the fact that ever since

the settlement of America the wolf has been pursued with guns, traps and poison, it is certain that no blow ever befel the race so severe as the extermination of the buffalo. Their natural prey gone, the wolves also in great measure disappeared. Probably they scattered out in search of food, and starved in great numbers. Those that survived were then forced to turn their attention to the herds of the stockmen, which furnished them an easy prey. They began to increase, and for years their depredations have resulted in very heavy loss to raisers of horses and cattle on the Northern plains.

As a rule, they do not attack the herds when alarmed and closely bunched together; but, prowling around the outskirts, they try to cut off the young stock, which is most easily killed. Sometimes, however, a small bunch of wolves may round up a little bunch of cattle, which stand in a close circle, their heads outward, prepared for the attack. After circling about them for a short time, two or three wolves will dash at the bunch, and if they can scatter the animals, it is the work of an instant only to pull down a yearling or kill two or three calves. Sometimes a single wolf, if it finds a two-year-old by itself, will run it down, and often by a single bite will kill it, or so disable it that its destruction is sure. Within the year I have come upon a two-year-old heifer killed in this way, by a single wolf — as the tracks in the snow showed—and by a single bite in the flank. There was more or less foam and saliva on the heifer's lips, and on the side of her neck and shoulders, showing that she had been chased some distance. When I rode up to the carcass it had been just killed, and was still bleeding and perfectly warm.

In the days of the buffalo, wolfing was a recognized industry, and one which was profitably followed. The method was simple. In winter, when the wolf skins were prime and when wolves were sure to be hungry, small parties of wolfers went to the buffalo range, and killed buffalo, which they poisoned with strychnine. This was usually not done until the cold weather had come and the ground was frozen, or, perhaps, covered with snow. The carcass of the buffalo used for bait was partly skinned, and then split, and more or less strychnine was placed in the visceral cavity, and mixed up there with entrails and

Drawn by Ernest Seton Thompson.　　THE GRAY WOLF.　　From "Forest and Stream."

blood, and into this strips of the meat were thrown. The remaining meat of the carcass was then thoroughly poisoned by scattering the strychnine over it, and this might even be rubbed into the flesh along with the warm blood taken from the hollow of the ribs. Often, while this was being done, the wolfer would be surrounded by a circle of ten or a dozen or more wolves, waiting patiently for him to complete his operations and go away, so that their meal might begin. In those days wolves had no fear of man. They were very seldom shot at, and knew of the gun chiefly as an implement to call them to a feast.

It was remarkable to see how quickly the wolves stripped the meat from the carcass of a buffalo; and the same thing, but in a less degree, can be seen to-day if a small bunch of wolves kill a range animal.

Facts bearing on these points are given by Joseph Kipp, an educated and thoroughly reliable Mandan half-breed, now nearly fifty years old, who was born and reared on the Missouri. In an interview quoted by Mr. J. W. Schultz in *Forest and Stream*, Mr. Kipp recently said:

"In the fall of 1864 the American Fur Company, at Fort Benton, sent me with a stock of trade goods to winter with the Piegans, who were camped on the Marias River. Early in February a man was sent out to assist me, and I lost no time in going on a hunt with the Indians, for I had been cooped up in a lodge all winter and wanted a change.

" One day we ran a large herd of buffalo, which we found a mile or two north of where Cutbank Stream joins the Marias. I had a splendid horse, but as soon as I killed a cow I stopped, for that was all the meat I wanted, and more too. I had reached the herd some time before the Indians did, and when they saw me dismount one of them asked me to exchange horses with him, as he wanted to make a big killing. I let him have it, and tying his horse to the horns of the buffalo, I proceeded to skin it. In less than five minutes the wolves began to gather about me. It was the running season, and each bitch was surrounded by a number of dog wolves playing and fawning about her, and quarreling with each other just like a lot of dogs. The wolves kept about fifty to sixty yards from me, but one coyote came up quite close, and a couple of kit foxes ventured up within eight or ten feet. I felt a little uneasy to be surrounded by such a big pack, and considered for some time whether to fire at them or not. I had only four balls left and rather wanted to keep them. Finally, however, I did shoot at a big white wolf, and not only killed him, but another one beyond. The rest of them, however, didn't pay any attention. Well, I only took the depouille and bossribs of the cow, and tying them on behind my saddle, I rode off about fifty yards. The wolves immediately ran up to the carcass, and such a snapping and clicking of teeth you never heard. In a very few minutes the cow was eaten up, and the bare bones were dragged and scattered about. The wolves, as soon as the carcass began to be fairly well picked, commenced striking out toward the northeast, and finally all of them went off in that direction, leaving only the kit foxes to keep me company. I cut off several bits of meat from the ribs tied to my saddle, and they would pounce on them almost before they struck the ground.

"In the old times wolves were much more numerous than coyotes, and to-day the conditions are directly the reverse. If wolves are

so much sharper and more difficult to catch
than coyotes, as some people say, how does it
happen that they are very scarce in the whole
West, while coyotes seem to be more numerous than they were in the old times?"

Conditions have changed for the wolf. In
early days he was disregarded, but now a very
large class of people in the West take an
active interest in wolves. As these animals
began to be troublesome, and to prey on the
stock of the cattlemen, people who had heard
of the old-time industry of wolfing took to
poisoning them, since, as a rule, the work of
trapping them called for more patience and
skill than the average ranchman possessed,
and they were too wary to be shot. At last,
however, the wolves refused to take the
poison; refused to eat any meat, in fact, except a carcass freshly killed by themselves.
This, of course, put an end to the poisoning,
and recourse was had again to steel traps.
With these, trappers have had some success.
I know of a case last winter where six wolves
were trapped in a very limited area, and, curiously enough, all of these were she wolves.
After people had become discouraged with
their lack of success in poisoning, a great

many greyhounds and staghounds were taken
into the West, and efforts were made to use
these to kill off the wolves on the ranges.
No doubt many wolves have been killed in
this way, as it is certain that many coyotes
have, but this method of hunting, while an
exhilarating sport, is inefficient as a means of
exterminating the wolves. In a level country
where the ground is good, dogs can overtake
and kill wolves; but they must be very swift
animals, regularly trained to the work, and
there must be two or three at least to each
wolf. I heard not long ago of a man who
started two wolf-hounds after a bunch of six
gray wolves, in a rough country. The dogs
easily overtook the wolves, which then turned
on them, and simply ate them up. In a
rough country dogs can accomplish but little
against the wolves, because they become footsore and hurt themselves against the stones,
and can no longer overtake the wolves. I
never heard of a wolf becoming footsore or
hurting himself among the rocks.

In the old buffalo days it was, of course, an
every-day matter for a man who was traveling
over the prairie to meet little bunches of five
or six or a dozen wolves strung out, traveling

one after another from place to place. These
seldom regarded the man any more than he
did them. Occasionally one might ride down
into a ravine, and almost over a wolf lying
asleep in some sunny spot or under a bush.
It would spring to its feet in great alarm,
make a half dozen wild jumps to some high
point, and stop for a look, and then, seeing
that it was only a man, would continue to
gaze, and at last trot unconcernedly away.
Nowadays it is rather unusual for any one
to see a wolf, and in recent times few men
have had such an experience as happened to
an acquaintance of mine, who, one morning in
April, 1897, stepped out of the cabin to look
about, when a big gray wolf came around the
corner of the house within fifteen feet of him.
Man and wolf were both astonished, and the
man jumped into the house to get his gun,
while the wolf ran to the top of a knoll about
two hundred yards away, and halted. When
it stopped the man shot, the ball entering the
right ham, ranging through the body, and
smashing the left shoulder. The wolf fell,
sprang to its feet again, and ran around in a
small circle, biting at the point where the ball
had hit it, while it yelled dismally, and so

loudly that it was heard at the next cabin, about two miles distant. The man cheered the ranch dog at the wolf, and jumped into the house again to put on his boots, for he had just gotten out of bed. By the time he had them on, and had started for the wolf, the dog came back with his face, breast and shoulders badly cut, though the wolf had seemingly made only two or three snaps at him. The man followed the wolf along the mountain side, over snowbanks, and up and down the sides of gulches for two miles, before he overtook it or could get a shot at it. All the time the animal was bleeding so freely that there was no difficulty in following the trail. When he came to it, it was too weak to go further, and he was able to finish it with stones.

In old times, the wolf in the buffalo range lived almost exclusively on the flesh of that animal, devouring the remains of those killed by the Indian or white hunters, and also those which perished by drowning, and by being mired in crossing streams. About the traps or " pounds," which were used by the Indians to catch buffalo, wolves were always abundant and fed upon the carcasses and remains left in the trap over night. If a band of buffalo were driven in toward evening, and the butchering was not finished that day, the wolves were sure to spoil whatever meat was left there during the night. It was, therefore, a common practice for the Indians to set snares in the openings of the fence which inclosed the buffalo corral, and in this way they caught many wolves. Another form of trap I have described in my book on the Blackfeet.* They also trapped many wolves by means of dead-falls, for in old times the fur of these animals was highly valued by some tribes for robes, and also for purposes of ornamentation, the buffalo robes often being trimmed with a margin of white wolf skin.

In countries where buffalo were not abundant, wolves killed for themselves and by running them down, deer, moose, caribou, and perhaps elk, though, as these last animals go in large droves in winter, it may be questioned whether the wolves often make successful attacks on them.

To-day the wolf feeds largely on domestic animals. On the western range it kills many colts, but chiefly calves and older cattle, as already described. The she wolf which has a

* " Blackfoot Lodge Tales," page 240.

litter of young puppies leaves them in their
home—usually a hole dug in some cut bank
or ravine—and, sallying out to the prey, eats
freely of its flesh, and then returning to the
mouth of the hole, disgorges the contents of
her stomach, on which the puppies feed. As
they are abundantly supplied, and do not con-
sume all that is brought to them, the immediate vicinity of the den is often very offensive
from the odor of the decaying flesh. We are
told that wolves change their abiding place
several times during the growth of a litter of
puppies.

The young wolves are born probably in
April, over most of the plains country. I
have seen them in July half grown, big and
strong, but as clumsy as pups at the same
age. I remember that once, many years ago,
as I rode down the valley of the Birdwood,
toward the North Platte, in company with
Major North and a dozen young fellows,
white and Indian, we startled from beneath a
bush an old she wolf and five half-grown puppies. There were two or three miles of level
bottom all about us, and our fresh horses
were eager for the race, which we were glad
to give them. We scattered out, and for a

little while the plain was alive with galloping
figures and noisy with cracking six-shooters,
and when we came together to resume our
ride, four of the wolf puppies had been accounted for, but the mother and the other
young one had escaped, either by speed or by
dodging into high grass, where it was impossible for us to find them.

In books on natural history tame wolves
are often mentioned, but I have never seen
one unconfined. I have, however, often seen
wolves, young and old, at play, when they
were ignorant of my presence, and have been
impressed by the similarity of their actions to
those of dogs under like circumstances. When
not alarmed, they often hold the tail high up.
I have seen them hold it nearly straight up,
and also curved up at various angles, as a dog
may hold his. To show affection or friendliness for their fellows, they wag their tails just
as a dog does; and some young wolves, seen
a year or two ago in the Zoölogical Park at
Washington, on the approach of the keeper
showed the evidences of affection and delight
that a dog would at the approach of a friend:
laying back their ears, grinning, wagging their
tails, and wriggling their bodies in an absurd

transport of joy. When the wolf is frightened, it tucks its tail between its legs, and forward under its belly, precisely as does a frightened dog.

A good many years ago a peculiar circumstance happened to me, which for a long time I was unable to explain to myself on any theory whatever. With a single companion I was traveling south through western Nebraska, then absolutely without inhabitants, and camped one night on the bare prairie, forty or fifty miles north of the Union Pacific Railroad. The night was moonless, but bright starlight, not at all what would be called a dark night. The horses were picketed close to us, and we had gone to bed, and were sleeping some few feet apart.

About the middle of the night I was awakened by feeling something drawn across my chest, and opening my eyes I saw, sitting on its haunches close to my body, a wolf, which, as I looked at it, reached out its paw and again drew it across my chest, much as a dog would scrape his paw over his master's knee if he wished to attract his attention. I was more or less irritated at being aroused, and, gently freeing my feet from the folds of the blanket about them, I threw one of them around and kicked the wolf in the ribs, when it promptly disappeared, and I saw nothing more of it.

I have since concluded that the wolf was uncertain whether it sat by a carcass or a living person, and was experimenting to satisfy itself on this point before beginning its meal. The animal was certainly a gray wolf, as shown by its size and outline, which I distinctly saw against the starlight sky, as well as by the resistance that I felt when my foot struck it, for it was not a small animal.

The wolf of Northern Europe is said to be a ferocious beast, and, when pressed by hunger in winter, frequently to destroy human beings. The wolf of North America, which is essentially the same animal, is notoriously a coward, and avoids man when he can. It is true that at frequent intervals stories appear in the newspapers giving accounts of attacks on human beings by wolves in this country. Such stories usually contain internal evidence of their falsity. Others on investigation have proved to be inventions, others still cannot be traced to their authors.

The fact seems to be that, until the advent

of white men in America, game was so plenty that the wolves had no difficulty in killing for themselves whatever they needed to supply their wants. They were seldom disturbed by man, and so were on terms of friendliness with the aborigines. Very soon after the coming of the white man the wolves began to learn that these new people were not friendly or indifferent, and were armed with weapons far more effective than those used by the Indians; and from regarding man as a friend and associate they came to avoid him as a being to be feared.

The deer, the moose, the caribou and the buffalo furnished a fat subsistence to the wolf, and long before those animals had become exterminated in any region, and hunger had forced him to consider the question of attacking human beings, the wolf had learned the power of the white man, and had retreated beyond the settlements to regions where game was still plenty.

Major Frank North, who, as a boy, in 1856 and '57, devoted a winter to poisoning wolves in Nebraska, and who followed the wild life of the western prairies almost up to the time of his death, nearly thirty years later, told me

173

that he had never in all his experience known of a wolf attacking a human being. On a number of occasions during the winter that he was poisoning wolves, when returning on foot after dark from putting out his baits, he was followed at a distance of not more than eight or ten feet by a huge white wolf. The first two or three times that it followed him he was afraid of it, believing that perhaps it might attack him, but it never approached very close to him.

I have known of but one person being attacked by a wolf, and this attack was apparently not made because the animal was hungry, but because it was cross. The person who was injured was a daughter of old Jim Baker, one of the few old-time trappers still living, who resides on Snake River, in the northwest corner of Colorado. The occurrence took place about sixteen years ago, and in summer. The young girl, then eighteen years old, went out just at dusk to drive in some milk cows. As she was going toward them, she saw a gray wolf sitting on the hillside, just above the trail. She shouted to frighten it away, and when it did not move, took up a stone and threw at it. The animal snarled at her call, and when she threw the stone came jumping down the hill, caught her by the shoulder, threw her down, and tore her badly on the arms and legs. She screamed, and her brother, who happened to be near and had his gun, ran up and killed the wolf. It was a young animal, barely full grown.

If a man is unarmed a wolf will often display great boldness. Only a few years ago, while on the Blackfoot Reservation, I rode past a wolf, perhaps forty yards distant, which did not even turn to look at me until I shouted at him. Then he slowly turned his head and looked at me, and actually seemed to grin. I had nothing about me more formidable than a jack-knife.

THE COYOTE

The range of the coyote extends from the Mississippi River to the Pacific Ocean, and as far north as to beyond the Red Deer's River, and south into Mexico. The coyote is a small animal, less than half the size of the gray wolf, and much more timid than that species, but it is abundant enough and intelligent enough to do a great deal of damage to the stockman's herds.

In old times, before the days of range cattle, the coyotes in the buffalo range subsisted chiefly on the dead buffalo that they found, on the remains of those killed by man, and of those killed by the wolves. In company with the gray wolves, the badgers and the kit foxes, they visited the Indian's buffalo traps. Besides this, they killed deer, antelopes, jack rabbits and grouse, together with prairie dogs, ground squirrels, mice, and all sorts of ground nesting birds. In those days coyotes seemed few in number by comparison with the gray wolves, and they were always timid. Yet at night they would sneak into camp, and carry away any food that might have been left lying about, or would chew up reins, horse collars, bridles, raw-hide ropes, and even saddles, if these were left where they could get at them.

In the northern plains country the young coyotes are born about May 1, and in their early puppyhood are maltese blue in color. They are brought forth usually in a hole dug in the side of a ravine, and until they are quite well grown do not venture far from home, holding themselves always in readiness to dive under ground at the slightest alarm.

From "Forest and Stream."

THE COYOTE.

Drawn by Ernest Seton Thompson.

Near the mouth of this hole may be found bones, feathers and bits of skin, and often the partially devoured bodies of rabbits, prairie dogs and gophers, on which the pups have been chewing or with which they have played. The parents are constantly foraging for them and they have plenty to eat.

Their retreat does not always save them, and I have more than once spent some hours in the hot sun in reaching the bottom of such a hole by laboriously digging into the bank with a butcher knife. If the inmates are captured the profit is not great, for their extreme timidity renders young coyotes most ill-natured, cantankerous and vicious pets. Their whole time and intelligence are devoted to solving the problem of escape, and usually one night—or at most two—gives them the solution, and they slip their collars, chew off their ropes, or gnaw a way out of the box, and in the morning are missing. Then everybody in camp—including him who held title to the beasts—is heartily glad to be rid of them.

If, however, the coyote can be captured very young, before it knows that there are such things as friends and enemies, it is readily tamed and makes an interesting, but always mischievous, pet. I have seen such tame coyotes—tame to their owners and to people that they were accustomed to see each day, but very shy to strangers, and keeping at a safe distance from them. An interesting group of three individuals seen on a ranch in northern Montana had been captured before their eyes were opened. As very small puppies they were tame, and very playful and pretty. When about half grown one disappeared, but the others remained about the place, on the best of terms with everyone, including the ten or a dozen greyhounds which were regularly used in hunting coyotes. A short time after this it was observed that the chickens were disappearing, and a little later their headless bodies would be found. A watch kept by the small boy who owned chickens and coyotes alike, proved that one of the wolves was killing the chickens for its own amusement, and one day while it was watching with keen satisfaction the struggles of a decapitated hen, the boy shot it.

The third member of the family grew to full size, and was a pretty, though timid, animal. It used to play gaily with the greyhound puppies of its own size, and evidently was perfectly at home with them. It wagged its tail and fawned on any one that it knew well who caressed it, but if a stranger attempted to pat it, it usually dodged, and would not come within reach of the hand. It did not always remain about the camp, but wandered away on to the prairie. Here it was several times seen, and taken for a wild coyote, and chased by the hounds. It would run fast and far, and at length, when tired or about to be overtaken, it would stop, lie down, and roll over on its back, lying there with its paws in the air until the pack came up. When the dogs reached it, and recognized it as a friend, it at once jumped up and fraternized with them, seeming by its actions to express its gratitude to them for having spared it, and, perhaps, its satisfaction at the joke it had played on the hounds. At all events, the boy who rode with the pack declared that he believed "the little devil done it a' purpose," and I was very much inclined to agree with him.

The wisdom of the coyote is proverbial. In the folk myths of many tribes of western Indians he is a mysterious and supernatural being, often one of the gods, but sometimes merely a man, whose craft and mysterious powers enable him to work wonders and to perform many marvelous deeds. Yet, whether god or man, he possesses a bad and malicious disposition, and is always getting into trouble, and constantly bringing misfortune on those with whom he is associated. The deeds attributed to the coyote by the Indians, while they pay a high tribute to his intelligence leave much to be desired as to his morals.

Coyotes do many curious things; but one of the oddest that I ever heard of was witnessed by my friend Captain North, at the old ranch on the Dismal River in northern Nebraska. The ranch house at the lake was built of sods or adobes, with walls eighteen inches or two feet thick. The window casings were set in the same plane with the inner walls, and the sashes were hinged above, and when the windows were open hooked to the ceilings of the rooms. There was thus at each window an embrasure as deep as the thickness of the wall, and as long and high as the sash.

Among the dogs at the ranch was a bull-terrier, which among the cow punchers there had a great reputation as a fighter, and was certainly the master of all the other dogs, and the boys never wearied of talking of his fighting qualities, or of wishing that he might meet some worthy foe.

One night in winter, some one happening to look out of the ranch window discovered, curled up close to the glass, a ball of fur, which a little inspection showed to be a coyote, which had jumped up into the embrasure, and was peacefully sleeping in the warm and sheltered place out of the wind and snow. The question at once arose what they should do with it. It could easily be killed, but there would be no fun in that. At length some genius among those present proposed that, while one man should cautiously open the window, another should stand by with the bull-terrier in his arms, and throw the bull-terrier on to the coyote. Then all could rush outside and witness the fight, and the dog's triumph. The plan was carried out. When all was ready the window was silently and swiftly opened and the dog was tossed on to the coyote, which at once disappeared, followed by the dog, and all hands rushed out to see the fight. They heard the dog rush barking around the house, and in a moment he passed them, and ran around the corner, barking and growling and greatly excited. Two or three times he ran about the house, but the coyote had disappeared, and at last all hands, much disappointed, went inside again. One of the men, going to the window to see that it was fastened, was astonished to see the coyote lying up against the glass, just as he had seen it a few moments before. The coyote had evidently jumped down from the window, run around the house, and when he came to the window again had jumped up into it and gone to sleep, as if nothing had happened.

The strangest part of the story follows. The dog was again thrown at the coyote, which at once repeated its performance, again completely baffling the dog, which lost all trace of it. It seems clear from this that the coyote, while smart enough to measure the dog's intelligence, did not connect the attack on him with the inside of the house, and probably did not know that the window had been opened. Such matters as a window and the inside of a house were, of course, quite outside the range of his experience. The cowboys, after this second attempt, being much impressed by the coyote's smartness, decided that he was entitled to undisturbed rest for the remainder of the night.

A year or two ago, while riding out to look at a bunch of cattle, I saw as I rode over a little hill near the house, a coyote down in the next valley, and with the coyote was a badger. I had no gun, and the coyote seemed to know it, for he paid no attention to me, but appeared to be playing with the badger. He would prance around it, make a feint of attacking it, and then run off a little way, the badger immediately running after him. This he did until the badger had gone sixty or seventy yards, when I got so near the two that the badger saw me, and ran into a hole, and the coyote trotted off a short distance, and lay down. This was not the first time that I had seen something like this going on, but I had never quite comprehended what it meant. Evidently the two animals were either playing with each other—which was most unlikely—or the wolf was teasing the badger. Further consideration, and talk with others who had seen the same thing, led me to believe that the wolf was plaguing the badger in order to make it follow him. The badger is notoriously short-tempered, and would rather fight than run away, and I have no doubt that the coyote's device was to make the badger so angry that it would follow him, and to draw it along until a second coyote was met with, when the two would attack the badger, and kill and eat it. In a fight, a badger would be more than a match for a single coyote, but two of them could probably tire him out, and at length kill him.

A striking example of craft and intelligence was seen last year (1896) at my ranch. We have there a rather worthless yellow sheep dog, which imagines that he can catch everything that runs away from him, and spends much time chasing coyotes, jack-rabbits, and antelope. He never catches any of these creatures, but he always chases them, and after he has run himself down, comes back with lolling tongue and a mortified air. The coyotes often in the daytime come up within one hundred and fifty or two hundred yards of the house, and whenever the dog sees them, he chases them out of sight. They do not appear to be very much afraid of him, and do not run away very fast. At night the coyotes come up close to the door, and can be heard all about the building, and at this time the dog is kept busy chasing them, but he does not follow them far after dark.

Not very long ago the coyotes devised a plan for getting rid of this dog. About nine o'clock at night, one of them came up close to the kitchen door and howled. The dog rushed out after it, and the coyote ran away down toward one of the corrals, and around behind the blacksmith's shop into the garden, the dog following after him at the top of his speed. Behind the blacksmith's shop were waiting six or seven other coyotes, which at once attacked the dog and began to worry him. The noise of the fight led Collins to seize his rifle and rush out there, and in the bright moonlight he saw a writhing, snarling mass of animals on the ground. At first he could not shoot for fear of killing the dog, but his shouts caused the coyotes to scatter, and he shot at one, but without result. He was only just in time to save the dog, which was badly cut up. Since that time Shep's interest in coyotes has somewhat abated. He still chases a single one with his old enthusiasm, but if a second appears he gives up the pursuit and returns to the house.

The coyote eats to live, and lives to eat,

and the question of subsistence occupies most of his thought. So he has become an expert in hunting methods, and these methods are well worth studying. It is in the manner in which these animals combine for mutual assistance in the actual chase that they show the greatest intelligence, securing with a minimum of effort creatures as swift as the jack-rabbit or the antelope.

Early in the spring, when the calves are being born, it is not unusual to see from one to three coyotes sitting round on the hills waiting for an old cow to hide her new-born calf and go off for water. At this time of the year they get a good many of the calves. It is not uncommon for several of them to surround a single cow with a young calf and try to kill it. They make fierce charges up close to the cow, in the hope of drawing her away from the calf, or frightening the calf so that it will leave her. If cow and calf had sense enough to keep close together there would be little danger, but often a young heifer will chase a coyote, and thus become separated from her calf, and then two or three bites from the other coyotes kill the calf.

I have several times seen this plan carried

out by coyotes, and that it is not confined to any one territory is shown by an account given by Miss Florence A. Merriam, in *Forest and Stream*, where she quotes a conversation with a California ranchman, which indicates that coyotes are everywhere very much alike. The man said to Miss Merriam:

"We used to miss our pigs when they were a month or six weeks old, and one day when I was carrying on the piling business I come out to the ranch and the hogs were up here, and I rode along, and as I got on to the rise where that black stump is," pointing out of the window toward the pasture fence, "I saw one of the old hogs chase a coyote. I thought it was a dog first, and stopped to see. Then I saw another coyote and the other hog was after him."

Two coyotes commonly work together, it is said; one to decoy the guardian of the young, while the other does the stealing.

"The little pigs was scart," the ranchman went on, "and they stood themselves up in a little pyramid pile while the old hogs was chasing the coyotes away. One coyote would come up and the hog would chase him, but the coyote would keep a-going to get the hog away from the pigs; bother and tease him to get him away. The other coyote would be dodgin' round close where the pigs were. Then the coyote that was furthest off he run and skipped by his hog, and run as fast as he could for the pile of pigs and got one. By the time the wolves had killed the pig, the old hogs were back after them, but they maneuvered round till one got the pig and dragged it off. Then the old hogs went after the other little pigs and took them to the hill."

"Have you ever seen the wolves chase a calf?" I asked the ranchman.

"Seen them?" he ejaculated. "I've seen them right there on that flat," pointing to the meadow below the house.

"There were two coyotes and a cow and a calf. The coyotes would both rush up together, and the cow would take after one, and he'd run off, and while she was chasing that one, the other one would slip up and kill the calf. If a coyote attacks one cow with a calf, when she sets up a-bawlin' all the cows within sight or hearing will come to the rescue, all bawlin' and bellerin' to drive you crazy."

The cowboys are greatly troubled by coyotes, and the farmer explained the reason by saying: "You know the cowboys here take a cow's hide and slit it up into strips and twist up a lariat for lassoing, and put a drag hondoo—a block of rawhide or wood—on the end. They picketed their horses out with them years ago when things was new, and often had their horses cut loose at night. The coyotes never bother rope, but I've seen rawhide lariats cut up into short pieces by them as slick and smooth as if cut with a knife. Everybody always looks out for his lariats when they are off on the ranges. A coyote would slip right up and cut them. I've been told of it by a great many horse men, and have heard of it out in the deserts east of here."

"They're a sneakin' animal," the ranchman declared, stroking his beard, and then went on to tell his experiences around the sheep camps. "If they get round the bed ground, the sheep will bunch up. I had a bunch of sheep, about 2,400, on the desert near the Grand Cañon. The coyotes was thick there. You could hear them barkin' in every direction—such gangs of them, all barking and howling at the same time. On a dark night like this they'd make night hideous. We were doctorin' the sheep for the scab, and had them all in a corral, and at night could hear them surging back and forth from one side to the other. The sheep men say coyotes never get inside a corral to get the sheep, but get close to the outside. When they get inside an inclosure they haven't much show to get out with anything—they're a sensible animal. But they're awful bold in the daytime when the sheep are out in the herd. They'll run up to one and cut its throat. Then there's a grand scatterin'," he concluded, as he reached for his hat, and went out to hitch the bucking broncho. So writes Miss Merriam.

The prong-horned antelope is the swiftest animal on the plains, and yet the coyotes catch a good many of them just by running them down. This sounds like a paradox, yet it is quite true, and is explained by the cunning of the wolves and the habits of the antelope.

A single coyote which undertook to run down a single antelope would get tired and hungry before he accomplished much, but when two or three coyotes are together it is quite a different thing. The coyotes do not all run after the antelope together. They take turns, and while one runs the others rest, and at last they tire the antelope out, and capture it.

If, when it was started, the antelope ran straight away, it would, of course, leave all the wolves behind, those that were resting even more than the one that was chasing it; but the antelope often does not run straight away; it is much more likely to run in large circles, and this enables the wolves to take turns when chasing it.

When three or four prairie wolves decide that they want antelope meat, one of them creeps as close as possible to the antelope they have selected, and makes a rush for it, running as fast as he possibly can, so as to push the antelope to its best speed and to tire it out. Meantime his companions spread out on either side of the runner, and get upon little hills or knolls so as to keep the chase in sight. They trot from point to point, and pretty soon, when the antelope turns and begins to work back toward one of them, this one tries to get as nearly as possible in its path, and as it flies by, the wolf dashes out at it and runs after it at top speed, while the one that had been chasing the antelope stops running and trots off to some nearby hill, where, while the water drips off his lolling tongue, he watches the race, and gets his breath again. After a little, the antelope passes near another coyote, which in turn takes up the pursuit. And so the chase is kept up until the poor antelope is exhausted, when it is overtaken and pulled down by one or more of the hungry brutes. Of course the coyotes do not catch every antelope they start. Sometimes the game runs such a course that it does not pass near any of the waiting wolves, and only the one that starts it has any running to do. In such a case the pursuit is soon abandoned. Sometimes the antelope is so stout and strong that it tires out all its pursuers.

Yet the wolves catch them more frequently than one would think, and it is not at all uncommon to see coyotes chasing antelope, although, of course, to see the whole race and its termination is very unusual. Often if a wolf running an antelope comes near to a man he gives up the chase, and that particular antelope is saved. It is a common thing for a coyote to chase an old doe with her kids just after the little ones have begun to run about. At that time they are very swift for short distances, but have not the strength to stand a long chase. In such a case a mother will often stay behind her young, and will try to fight off the coyote, butting him with her head and striking him with her forefeet. He pays little attention to her, except to snap at her, and keeps on after the kids. Several times I have seen a mother antelope lead her little ones into the midst of a bed of cactus, where the wolf could not go without getting his feet full of thorns. If the bed is small, the wolf makes ferocious dashes up to its border, trying to frighten the little ones so that they will run out on the other side and he can start after them again, but usually the mother has no trouble in holding them. I have several times killed young antelope whose legs had been bitten by coyotes, but which had got away.

The coyotes understand very well at what time of the year the young antelope are born, and at this season they spend much time sitting about on the hills and watching the old does. These, however, are often pretty well able to take care of themselves, and I have seen an old doe, which unquestionably had young hidden somewhere nearby in the grass, chase a coyote clear out of the county. She kept close behind him for the three-quarters of a mile that I could see them, striking at him as she ran, and he had his tail between his legs, and was evidently thoroughly scared.

One hot summer day some years ago, a gang of section men were working in a cut on the Union Pacific Railroad west of Laramie, when suddenly a big buck antelope ran down one side of the cut, across the track, and up the other side. His sudden dash in among them startled the men; and while they stood looking up where he had crossed, a coyote suddenly plunged down the side of the cut, just as the antelope had done. The readiest of the section men threw a hammer at him, and the wolf turned and scrambled up the bank that he had just come down, and was not seen again.

Some years ago I camped one afternoon on Rock Creek, Wyo., and as there was very little feed we turned the horses loose at night to pick among the sage brush and grease wood. Early in the morning, before sunrise, while the man with me was getting breakfast, I started out to look for the horses. They were nowhere to be seen, and I climbed to the top of the hill back of camp, from which, as it was the only high place anywhere about, I felt sure that I could see the missing animals. Just before I got to the top of the hill an old doe antelope suddenly came in view, closely followed by a coyote. Both of them seemed to be running as hard as they could, and both had their tongues hanging out as if they had come a long way. Suddenly, almost at the heels of the antelope—much closer to her than the other wolf—appeared a second coyote, which now took up the running, while the one that had been chasing her stopped, and sat down and watched. The antelope ran quite a long distance, always bearing a little to the left, and now seeming to run more slowly than when I first saw her. As she kept turning, it was evident that she would either run around the hill on which I stood or would come back near it. At first I was so interested in watching her that I forgot to look at the wolf that had halted near me. When I did so he was no longer at the place where he had paused, but was trotting over a little ridge that ran down from the hill, and watching the chase that was now so far off. He could easily have run across the cord of the arc and headed the antelope, but he knew too well what she would do to give himself that trouble. After a little, it was evident that the antelope would come back pretty near to the hill, but on the other side of it from where she had passed before, and the wolf which I had first seen chasing her trotted out two or three hundred yards on to the prairie and sat down. The antelope was now coming back almost directly toward him, and I could see that there were two wolves behind her, one close at her heels and the other a long way further back. The first wolf now seemed quite excited. He no longer sat up, but crouched close to the ground, every few moments raising his head very slowly to take a look at the doe, and then lowering it again, so that he would be out of sight. Sometimes he crawled on his belly a few feet further from me, evidently trying to put himself directly in the path of the antelope; and this he seemed to have succeeded in doing. As she drew near him I could see that she was staggering, she was so tired, and the wolf behind could at any moment have knocked her down if he had wanted to, but he seemed to be waiting for something. The wolf that was following him was now running faster and catching up.

When the antelope reached the place where the first wolf was lying hidden, he sprang up, and in a jump or two caught her by the neck and threw her down. At the same moment the two wolves from behind came up, and for a moment there was a scuffle, in which yellow and white and gray and waving tails were all mixed up, and then the three wolves were seen standing there, tearing away at their breakfast.

I was so much interested in the intelligence shown by the coyotes that I do not think I felt the least sympathy for the antelope. Even if I had wanted to help her I could have done nothing, for she was so tired that the coyotes could easily have caught her after I had gone.

Mr. Lew Wilmot, an old-timer in the Western country, has contributed to *Forest and Stream* some interesting notes on the hunting habits of the coyote, which are well worth quoting. He says:

" A few years ago along in the spring, I took my rifle and started up into the open hills to kill some grouse, and when I got up on the top of a small ridge that puts down between my creek and the Columbia River, I stood still for a while, listening for a grouse to hoot.

"Across from where I stood was quite a high mountain, covered with bunch grass and a few scattering pines; the snow had not all gone, especially near the top. I had not stopped very long when I saw a deer coming over the hill, and from the way it was running I knew there was something after it. Soon I saw two coyotes down to the right, and from the way they were running I thought they were trying to head the deer off from the river. Soon I saw two more on the trail, and then I saw two more to the left, and it looked to me as if those that were on the flanks were running the fastest. There was a crossing in a gap in the ridge I was on, and I knew the deer would come through that gap; so I ran down toward the gap, not that I wanted to shoot the deer, but I wanted to shoot at the coyotes that were on the deer's track.

"I had not got quite down to the gap when the deer came through. It was a whitetail buck, and he was doing his best to get to the river. I had but a short time to wait when the two coyotes came along. I whistled when they got opposite to me and they stopped and looked up. I fired at the one that looked the largest. At the crack of the rifle it started, and ran as fast as it could for about fifty yards and rolled over dead. The other followed it for a few yards and then turned off up the hill, and when it saw its mate roll over it stopped. I shot at it, and as I did not make the right allowance for distance, undershot and broke one of its legs. I put my dog after it and he soon brought it to bay, and I had the satisfaction of killing it.

"On another occasion I was coming down from a neighbor's, and when near the bottom on the Columbia I noticed a couple of coyotes hunting through the grass and low bushes; they had their tails up like dogs, and seemed to be as busy.

"Soon they were joined by two more, and all had their tails up, and as they had not discovered me I waited to see what they were after. I never saw dogs hunt through a flat more diligently than they did, and it was very amusing to see them with their tails up. I think they were hunting chipmunks. Not having anything to shoot with, I started on, and when they saw me they trotted off up the gulch, but lowered their tails, coyote-like.

"I have often been told by white men and

by Indians that they have seen as many as fifteen coyotes after one deer. This winter while on a trip to Curlew I had to go down on Kettle River, and I saw where six deer had been caught by coyotes. I examined to see whether any big wolves had been among them, but did not see a track. An old Indian told me that a few days before the coyotes had run a deer down on to the ice and caught it, and he heard it bleat, and he ran down, but when he got there they had almost eaten it up."

Accounts of how the coyote points the game that it is hunting have often been published, and one summer during haying time a good example of this was seen by some of the hay-makers at my ranch in Wyoming.

The loaded hay wagon was coming back from one of the meadows, when a coyote was seen forty or fifty yards from the road apparently on a stiff point. He was standing absolutely still, his nose and tail straight out in a line, and one forefoot lifted from the ground. Just before him there was a very slight rise of ground, but the men who were riding on top of the load of hay could see over this, and saw that he was pointing a prairie dog which was feeding near its hole, just on the other side of the elevation. They were so interested in the sight that they stopped the wagon and watched. Every little while the prairie dog would sit up and look about, and when he did this the coyote would stand absolutely without motion. When the dog dropped down on all four feet and began to feed, the coyote would very slowly and stealthily creep up a few feet nearer. This thing went on for some minutes, the dog not seeming to notice the coyote, which at the last must have been in plain sight. The last time the dog dropped down to feed, the coyote made a swift rush, covering twelve or fifteen feet, picked the little animal up, and then for the first time noticing the hay wagon, stood for a moment with his prey hanging across his mouth, and then trotted slowly off up the hill.

As he is usually seen, the coyote gives one the impression of a down-trodden much-bullied animal, that desires nothing so much as to get away. It sneaks along with downcast mien and lowered tail, and casts fearful glances backward over its shoulder, as if it expected every moment to have a stone thrown at it. But if you happen to be without a gun when you meet it, there is no animal on the prairie more unconcerned and impudent. They will bark at you from a nearby hilltop, or trot a few paces from the trail you are following, and lie down and yawn as you ride by with an assumption of being bored that would be aggravating if it were not so comical.

Their impudence shows itself sometimes in their daring to tease the big wolves, whose power one would think should protect them from such attacks. A pair of coyotes were seen one winter not long ago, on a big piece of ice, engaged in bothering a gray wolf. The ice was slippery, and they could get started and could turn much more quickly than their larger cousin. One of them would dance in front of him and annoy him, while the other ran by from behind and nipped him as it went past. Then the big wolf would try to turn and chase the little one, but he would slip, and before he fairly got started would get a nip from the other. So they worried him for a long time—in fact, until the observer tired of looking at them, and rode away.

To my mind the coyote is a much more interesting animal than the gray wolf, and I believe that on account of his greater abundance and his far greater intelligence he does almost as much harm. On the other hand, he does not a little good by killing prairie dogs, ground squirrels, and other rodents that destroy the farmers' crops.

I never see a coyote nowadays without being reminded of my old friend Medicine Bear, and of the speech he addressed to me in a council with reference to his support in the future. He began something like this :

I always think about living. If I was thinking of dying I would have been dead long ago. I like to eat and that is why I am living, and when I see you out here, I see that I can still live, and that I am still going to have some more meat. The only thing I am living for now is eating. Ever since I have been living there has not been a day of this time but I have had something to eat, so it makes me feel good when I hear a man talking about how I can still live.

George Bird Grinnell.

On the Little Missouri

Formerly the prong-horned antelope were very plentiful on the immense rolling prairies which stretch back of the Little Missouri, where my ranch house stands. In the old days they could often be procured by luring them with a red flag — for they are very inquisitive beasts. Now they have grown scarce and wary, and must usually either be stalked, which is difficult, owing to their extreme keenness of vision and the absence of cover on the prairies, or else must be ridden into. With first-class greyhounds and good horses they can often be run down in fair chase; without greyhounds the rider can hope for nothing more than to get within fair shooting-range, and this only by taking advantage of their peculiarity of running straight ahead in the direction in which they are pointed when once they have settled into their pace. Usually antelope, as soon as they see a hunter, run straight away from him;

but sometimes they make their flight at an
angle, and as they do not like to change their
course when once started, it is occasionally
possible to cut them off from the point toward
which they are headed, and get a reasonably
close shot.

In the fall of 1896 I spent a fortnight on
the range with the ranch wagon. I was using
for the first time one of the new small-calibre,
smokeless-powder rifles, a 30-30-160 Winchester. I had a half-jacketed bullet, the butt
being cased in hard metal, while the nose was
of lead.

While traveling to and fro across the range
we usually moved camp each day, not putting
up the tent at all during the trip; but at one
spot we spent three nights. It was in a creek
bottom, bounded on either side by rows of
grassy hills, beyond which stretched the rolling prairie. The creek bed, which at this
season was of course dry in most places,
wound in S-shaped curves, with here and
there a pool and here and there a fringe
of stunted wind-beaten timber. We were
camped near a little grove of ash, box-elder,
and willow, which gave us shade at noonday;
and there were two or three pools of good

water in the creek bed—one so deep that I
made it my swimming-bath.

The first day that I was able to make a
hunt I rode out with my foreman, Sylvane
Ferris. I was mounted on Muley. Twelve
years before, when Muley was my favorite
cutting pony on the round-up, he never
seemed to tire or lose his dash, but Muley
was now sixteen years old, and on ordinary
occasions he liked to go as soberly as possible; yet the good old pony still had the fire
latent in his blood, and at the sight of
game—or, indeed, of cattle or horses—he
seemed to regain for the time being all the
headlong courage of his vigorous and supple
youth.

On the morning in question it was two or
three hours before Sylvane and I saw any
game. Our two ponies went steadily forward
at a single foot or shack, as the cow-punchers
term what Easterners call "a fox trot." Most
of the time we were passing over immense
grassy flats, where the mat of short curled
blades lay brown and parched under the
bright sunlight. Occasionally we came to
ranges of low barren hills, which sent off
gently rounded spurs into the plain.

On the Little Missouri

It was on one of these ranges that we first saw our game. As we were traveling along the divide we spied eight antelope far ahead of us. They saw us as soon as we saw them, and the chance of getting to them seemed small; but it was worth an effort, for by humoring them when they start to run, and galloping toward them at an angle oblique to their line of flight, there is always some little chance of getting a shot. Sylvane was on a light buckskin horse, and I left him on the ridge crest to occupy their attention while I cantered off to one side. The prong-horns became uneasy as I galloped away, and ran off the ridge crest in a line nearly parallel to mine. They did not go very fast, and I held in Muley, who was all on fire at the sight of the game. After crossing two or three spurs, the antelope going at half speed, they found I had come closer to them, and turning, they ran up one of the valleys between two spurs. Now was my chance, and wheeling at right angles to my former course, I galloped Muley as hard as I knew how up the valley nearest and parallel to where the antelope had gone. The good old fellow ran like a quarter-horse, and when we were almost at the main ridge crest I leaped off, and ran ahead with my rifle at the ready, crouching down as I came to the sky-line. Usually on such occasions I find that the antelope have gone on, and merely catch a glimpse of them half a mile distant, but on this occasion everything went right. The band had just reached the ridge crest about 220 yards from me across the head of the valley, and had halted for a moment to look around. They were starting as I raised my rifle, but the trajectory is very flat with these small-bore smokeless-powder weapons, and taking a coarse front sight I fired at a young buck which was broadside to me. There was no smoke, and as the band raced away I saw him sink backward, the ball having broken his hips.

We packed him bodily behind Sylvane on the buckskin and continued our ride, as there was no fresh meat in camp, and we wished to bring in a couple of bucks if possible. For two or three hours we saw nothing. The unshod feet of the horses made hardly any noise on the stretches of sun-cured grass, but now and then we passed through patches of thin weeds, their dry stalks rattling curiously, making a sound like that of a rattlesnake. At last, coming over a gentle rise of ground, we spied

two more prong-bucks, half a mile ahead of us
and to our right.

Again there seemed small chance of bagging
our quarry, but again fortune favored us. I at
once cantered Muley ahead, not toward them,
but so as to pass them well on one side. After
some hesitation they started, not straight away,
but at an angle to my own course. For some
moments I kept at a hand gallop, until they
got thoroughly settled in their line of flight;
then I touched Muley, and he went as hard
as he knew how. Immediately the two panic-
stricken and foolish beasts seemed to feel that
I was cutting off their line of retreat, and raced
forward at mad speed. They went much faster
than I did, but I had the shorter course, and
when they crossed me they were not fifty yards
ahead—by which time I had come nearly a
mile. At the pull of the rein Muley stopped
short, like the trained cow-pony he is; I leaped
off, and held well ahead of the rearmost and
largest buck. At the crack of the little rifle
down he went with his neck broken. In a
minute or two he was packed behind me on
Muley, and we bent our steps toward camp.

During the remainder of my trip we were
never out of fresh meat, for I shot three other

bucks—one after a smart chase on horseback, and the other two after careful stalks; and I missed two running shots.

The game being both scarce and shy, I had to exercise much care, and after sighting a band I would sometimes have to wait and crawl round for two or three hours before they would get into a position where I had any chance of approaching. Even then they were more apt to see me and go off than I was to get near them.

Antelope are the only game that can be hunted as well at noonday as in the morning or evening, for their times for sleeping and feeding are irregular. They never seek shelter from the sun, and when they lie down for a noonday nap they are apt to choose a hollow, so as to be out of the wind; in consequence, if the band is seen at all at this time, it is easier to approach them than when they are up and feeding. They sometimes come down to water in the middle of the day, sometimes in the morning or evening. On this trip I came across bands feeding and resting at almost every time of the day. They seemed usually to feed for a couple of hours, then begin feeding again.

The last shot I got was when I was out with Joe Ferris, in whose company I had killed my first buffalo, just thirteen years before, and not very far from this same spot. We had seen two or three bands that morning, and in each case, after a couple of hours of useless effort, I failed to get near enough. At last, toward mid-day, after riding and tramping over a vast extent of broken sun-scorched country, we got within range of a small band lying down in a little cup-shaped hollow in the middle of a great flat. I did not have a close shot, for they were running about 180 yards off. The buck was rearmost, and at him I aimed; the bullet struck him in the flank, coming out of the opposite shoulder, and he fell in his next bound. As we stood over him, Joe shook his head, and said, "I guess that little .30-30 is the ace"; and I told him I guessed so to.

Beside antelope, the only wild beasts of any size which are still left on the plains anywhere near the Little Missouri are wolves and coyotes. Coyotes are more or less plentiful everywhere in thinly settled districts. They are not dangerous to horses or cattle, but they will snap up lambs, young pigs, cats, and hens, and if very hungry several often combine to attack a young calf. In consequence, farmers and ranchers kill them whenever the chance offers ; but they do no damage which is very appreciable when compared with the ravages of their grim big brother, the gray wolf, which in many sections of the West is now a veritable scourge of the stock-men.

The big wolves shrink back before the growth of the thickly settled districts, and in the Eastern States they often tend to disappear even from districts that are uninhabited, save by a few wilderness hunters. They have thus disappeared almost entirely from Maine, the Adirondacks, and the Alleghanies, although here and there they are said to be returning to their old haunts. Their disappearance is rather mysterious in some instances, for they are certainly not all killed off. The black bear is much easier killed, yet the black bear holds its own in many parts of the land from which the wolf has vanished. No animal is quite so difficult to kill as is the wolf, whether by poison or rifle or hound. Yet, after a comparatively few have been slain, the entire species will perhaps vanish from certain localities.

But with all wild animals, it is a noticeable fact that a course of contact with man continu-

ing over many generations of animal life causes
a species so to adapt itself to its new surroundings that it ceases to diminish in numbers.
When white men take up a new country, the
game, and especially the big game, being entirely unused to contend with the new foe,
succumbs easily, and is almost completely
killed out. If any individuals survive at all,
however, the succeeding generations are far
more difficult to exterminate than were their
ancestors, and they cling much more tena-
ciously to their old homes. The game to be
found in old and long-settled countries is much
more wary and able to take care of itself than
the game of an untrodden wilderness. It is a
very difficult matter to kill a Swiss chamois;
but it is a very easy matter to kill a white goat
after a hunter has once penetrated among the
almost unknown peaks of the mountains of
British Columbia. When the ranchmen first
drove their cattle to the Little Missouri they
found the deer tame and easy to kill, but the
deer of Maine and the Adirondacks test to the
full the highest skill of the hunter.

In consequence, after a time, game may even
increase in certain districts where settlements
are thin. This has been true of the wolves

throughout the northern cattle country in Montana, Wyoming, and the western ends of the Dakotas. In the old days wolves were very plentiful throughout this region, closely following the huge herds of buffaloes. The white men who followed these herds as professional buffalo-hunters were often accompanied by other men, known as wolfers, who poisoned these wolves for the sake of their furs. With the disappearance of the buffalo the wolves diminished in numbers so that they also seemed to disappear. During the last ten years their numbers have steadily increased, and now they seem to be as numerous as they ever were in the region in question, and they are infinitely more wary and more difficult to kill.

Along the Little Missouri their ravages have been so serious during the past four years as to cause heavy damage to the stock-men. Not only colts and calves, but young trail stock, and in midwinter even full-grown horses and steers, are continually slain ; and in some seasons the losses have been so heavy as to more than eat up all the profits of the ranchman. The county authorities have put a bounty on wolf scalps of three dollars each, and in my own neighborhood the ranchmen have of their own accord put on a further bounty of five dollars. This makes eight dollars for every wolf, and as the skin is also worth something, the business of killing wolves is quite profitable.

Wolves are very shy, and show extraordinary cunning both in hiding themselves and in slinking out of the way of the hunter. They are rarely killed with the rifle. I have myself shot but one with the rifle, though I have several times taken part in the chase of a wolf with dogs, and have if necessary helped the pack finish the quarry. They are occasionally trapped, but after a very few have been procured in this way the survivors become so wary that it is almost impossible even for a master of the art to do much with them, while an ordinary man can never get one into a trap except by accident. More can be done with poison, but even in this case the animal speedily learns caution by experience. When poison is first used in a district wolves are very easily killed, and perhaps most of them will be slain, but nowadays it is difficult to catch any but young ones in this way. Occasionally an old one will succumb, but there are always some who cannot be persuaded to touch a bait. The old she-wolves teach their cubs, as soon as they are able to walk, to avoid man's trace in every way, and to look out for traps and poison.

In consequence, though most cow-punchers carry poison with them, and are continually laying out baits, and though some men devote most of their time to poisoning for the sake of the bounty and the fur, the results are not very remunerative. The most successful wolf-hunter on the Little Missouri for the past year was a man who did not rely on poison at all, but on dogs. He is a hunter named Massingale, and he always has a pack of at least twenty hounds. The number varies, for a wolf at bay is a terrible fighter, with jaws like that of a steel trap and teeth that cut like knives, so that the dogs are continually disabled and sometimes killed, and the hunter has always to be on the watch to add animals to his pack. It is not a pack that would appeal, as far as looks go, to an Old-World huntsman, but it is thoroughly fitted for its own work. Most of the dogs are greyhounds, whether rough or smooth haired, but many of them are big mongrels, part greyhound and part some other breed, such as bull-dog, mastiff, Newfoundland, bloodhound, or collie. The only two requisites are that the dogs shall run fast and fight gamely; and in consequence they form as wicked, hard-biting a crew as ever ran down and throttled a wolf. They are usually taken out ten at a time, and by their aid Massingale killed two hundred wolves during the year. Of course there is no pretence of giving the game fair play. The wolves are killed as vermin, not for sport. The greatest havoc is in the spring-time, when the she-wolves are followed to their dens, which are sometimes holes in the earth and sometimes natural caves. There are from three to nine whelps in each litter. Some of the hounds are very fast, and they can usually overtake a young or weak wolf; but an old dog-wolf, with a good start, unless run into at once, will surely get away if he is in running trim. Frequently, however, he is caught when he is not in running trim, for the hunter is apt to find him when he has killed a calf or taken part in dragging down a horse or steer, and is gorged with meat. Under these circumstances he cannot run long before the pack.

If possible, as with all such packs, the

hunter himself will get up in time to end the worry by a stab of his hunting-knife; but unless he is quick he will have nothing to do, for the pack is thoroughly competent to do its own killing. Grim fighter though a great dog-wolf is, he stands no show before the onslaught of ten such hounds, agile and powerful, who rush on their antagonist in a body. They possess great power in their jaws, and unless Massingale is up within two or three minutes after the wolf is taken, the dogs literally tear him to pieces, though one or more of their number may be killed or crippled in the fight.

Other hunters are now striving to get together packs thoroughly organized, and the wolves may soon be thinned out; but at present they are certainly altogether too plentiful. Last fall I saw a number myself, although I was not looking for them. I frequently came upon the remains of sheep and young stock which they had killed, and once, on the top of a small plateau, I found the body of a large steer, while the torn and trodden ground showed that he had fought hard for his life before succumbing. There were apparently two wolves engaged in the work, and the cunning beasts had evidently acted in concert. While one attracted the steer's attention, the other, according to the invariable wolf habit, attacked him from behind, hamstringing him and tearing out his flanks. His body was still warm when I came up, but his murderers had slunk off, either seeing or smelling me. Their handiwork was unmistakable, however, for, unlike bears and cougars, wolves invariably attack their victim at the hindquarters, and begin their feast on the hams or flanks if the animal is of any size.

It will be noticed that in some points my observations about wolves are in seeming conflict with those of Mr. Grinnell; but I think the conflict is more seeming than real; and in any event I have concluded to let the article stand just as it is. The great book of Nature contains many passages which are hard to read, and at times conscientious students may well draw up different interpretations of the obscurer and least known texts. It may not be that either observer is at fault; but what is true of an animal in one locality may not be true of the same animal in another, and even in the same locality two individuals of a species may widely differ in their habits. On the

Little Missouri, for the last two or three years, as formerly on the Sun River, hunting with dogs has been found to be a far more successful method of getting rid of wolves than trapping. Doubtless there are places where this would not be true. I am inclined to think that wherever wolves have been chased in one manner for a long time, a new method will at first prove particularly efficacious. When they have become thoroughly used to poison, traps have a great success. If they are persistently trapped, then poisoning does well.

I am particularly interested in what Mr. Grinnell's informants have described as to the occasional tolerance, even by hungry wolves, of kit foxes; for frequently a wolf will snap up a fox as quickly as he would a fawn, and once, at least, I have known of a coyote being killed by a wolf for food.

Theodore Roosevelt.

NOTE.—The apparent discrepancies between the observations recorded in the two articles on wolves just preceding, may, we think, readily be explained on two grounds. One of these is that of difference in locality, but more important is the difference in the date of the two sets of observations. In the West, difference in time means difference in surrounding conditions.

On the Little Missouri

It is suggested that two points in Mr. Grinnell's article are open to criticism. It is known that to-day hungry wolves will readily kill foxes, and Mr. Grinnell himself gives examples of what he believes to be attempts by coyotes to kill badgers. Therefore, the account quoted from Mr. Kipp, of a pair of hungry wolves mingled with coyotes and kit foxes, waiting near a buffalo carcass, seems almost incredible. The wolves should have eaten the kit foxes, and, perhaps, even the coyotes.

The answer to this is simple. At the time to which the event here quoted refers, wolves were never hungry. We are accustomed in a conventional way to speak of wolves as lean and hungry beasts, but in the buffalo days they were seldom or never lean, and seldom or never really hungry, because they always had plenty of buffalo meat. Therefore, it was that wolves, coyotes, badgers and kit foxes associated on terms of more or less equality, and very seldom, so far as known, interfered with each other. Of course, at a feast the big wolves served themselves first, and the other animals came after them in order of size, unless there was enough for all, which was usually the case. To-day the big wolves are glad to eat any animal smaller than themselves. Coyotes try to catch and eat badgers and kit foxes, and it is possible that occasionally in some way the badger may be able to capture and eat a kit fox. For all these animals food now is very scarce. For all of them, food in the old times was extremely abundant.

It is further suggested that the statement that wolves regarded the Indians as friends, is putting it a little too strongly, since it is also stated that many tribes assiduously hunted them for their fur. It is true that the

Indians caught wolves for their skins, but they did not pursue them, that is to say, they did not—or very seldom—shoot at them or chase them. They caught them in traps and snares, and the wolves, being usually full fed and seldom or never frightened by the Indians, were exceedingly tame. Note, in confirmation of this view, a statement in "Lewis and Clark's Travels," page 172 (Longman, London, 1814), where the wolves about a buffalo trap are said to have been very fat, and so "gentle that one of them was killed with an esponton."

When Mr. Grinnell makes a general statement about how wolves and Indians regard each other, he confesses that he is generalizing about all Indians and all wolves from those Indians and those wolves that he has known. Very likely he may be wrong as to certain sections of the country, but he is convinced that he is right so far as the plains country and the buffalo Indians were concerned. On the other hand, in one of the old books about British Columbia, where there were no buffalo, wolves are said to be always hungry, and mention is made of the havoc these animals wrought among horses, and of the fact that they occasionally attacked men, so that the Indians stood in dread of them. Statements about hungry wolves, and wolves attacking men, must, however, be accepted with caution.

No fact in natural history is better ascertained than that wild animals adapt themselves with extraordinary rapidity to the new conditions which they have to face on the settling up of a country. This fact will often explain the conflicting statements made by observers in different places and at different times.

The Editors.

Bear Traits

Bears are recognized as the shyest and wariest of big animals, but most of the stories told about them have to do more with the emotions of the hunter, or with the game's ferocity when wounded, than with the manner of life of the bear. The increasing scarcity and increasing shyness of these animals renders the study of their habits each year more difficult, and it is high time that observations such as here set down should be recorded.

A BERRY PICKER

It was on a little river flowing into the head of a British Columbia inlet that I saw my first bear—a black one. We had laboriously poled our canoe for a mile or two up the rushing river, and had landed on a gravel bar to survey the mountain sides for white goats, when around a point a little below us on the other side of the stream walked a moderate sized bear. It was August, and the ripe salmon berries hung thick on bushes which grew in the edge of the forest on the cut bank beneath which the river flowed. These berries occupied all the bear's attention, and he did not notice the men who stood in plain sight on the other side of the stream. He walked slowly along from bush to bush, raising his head and wrapping his tongue around the branches, and then stripping off berries and leaves alike by a downward pull. When he had cleared the lower branches, he stood on his hind feet, and pulling down the higher branches with his forepaws, he stripped them in the same way. All his motions were deliberate, and the way in which he gathered the food with mouth and tongue reminded me of a cow pulling apples from a low-growing tree.

I watched him with great interest until he had approached within perhaps seventy-five yards of where we stood. Then, fearing that he would smell us, I fired at the white spot in his breast, and, as the smoke lifted, had a dissolving view of his hips as they disappeared in the undergrowth. When we had pushed across the river in the canoe, we found blood on the weeds where he had vanished, and a little further in the forest came upon the bear, comfortably curled up on his side with his paws over his nose.

Bear Traits

Once in Montana, at a much greater distance, I saw an old bear and two cubs picking huckleberries in a little mountain valley. They walked busily about from bush to bush and seemed to gather the berries one by one, though the distance was too great for me to be sure as to this. The Indians tell me that when the service berries are ripe, the bears "ride" down the taller bushes by their weight, pressing the stems down under the chest, the two forelegs being on either side of the stem. I have seen quite stout service berry trees that had evidently been borne down in precisely this way.

George Bird Grinnell.

A SILVER TIP FAMILY

Most of my hunting of grizzlies was in the Big Horn Mountains, in 1880, 1881, 1882, and 1883, at a time when they were not much disturbed, and had not as yet adopted what I understand is now a common habit, of feeding almost exclusively at night. A favorite custom of mine was to ride to a hill or point overlooking a good deal of hillside and forest margin, picket my hunting pony, and with a good field-glass to watch such game as might appear ; and in those days it was seldom that some animals were not in sight—buffalo, elk, white tail or mule deer, antelope, sheep, and black or silver tip bears—according to the locality. As a rule, I preferred to watch rather than to hunt, unless an unusually fine head or the need of meat in camp was an incentive to kill. Of the game seen none was more interesting than the silver tip, and with one family I became quite well acquainted.

While on a fishing trip in June, camp was made on a fine trout stream where I passed several days, fishing a little and incidentally looking over the country with a view to returning in October for a fall hunt. Near by was a divide, open for a mile or more and then covered with pines, surrounded on two sides of its triangle by small cañons. Regularly each afternoon about four o'clock, a large female silver tip with two cubs would appear from the woods and work over the ground, sometimes till dark. Occasionally a larger bear, probably a male, would appear, but did not join the others, who seemed to be rather afraid of him. I may mention that on one occasion three mule deer crossed the slope a little below the bears, so that I had the unusual experience of having four bears and three deer in the field of the glass at one time.

The chief occupation of the bears while in sight was turning over stones in search of insects beneath, and it was most interesting to watch their methods. A man turning over a stone usually draws it over directly toward himself, to the imminent danger of his toes; but a bear knows better than that. In the case of a heavy stone, they would brace themselves with one foreleg and with the other raise the stone and give it an outward sweep well to one side, so that it would not strike them in falling. The moment the stone was over their heads went down, and they apparently licked up such insects as were in sight, though I was not near enough actually to see this. Then usually one or two rapid sweeps of a paw were made, probably to uncover such insects as might have secreted themselves. One of the cubs would sometimes join the mother in this search, but generally each worked independently. Imitating their mode of search, I have found many beetles and ants, and numbers of mole crickets, and of the large stone cricket (*Anabrus*). In this place, at least, dead stumps were rarely searched.

The habit of turning over stones is very general in the spring and early summer, and was one of the best indications of the presence of bears; later in the season, wild plums and other fruits are more generally sought as food. This family of bears were regular in their habits, feeding from early morning till about nine o'clock, and reappearing about four in the afternoon. On cloudy or showery days they might be seen at intervals all day, but a hard rain they avoided. The female, while watchful, was not at all shy. She happened to be in sight when the tents were pitched, a process she watched with much apparent interest and some surprise. At first she brought her cubs in close to her; but before long they resumed their search for insects, and finding they were not molested, paid little more attention to us. When watching an object she would raise herself to her full height on her forelegs and elevate the head, which was moved slowly from side to side, giving her a rather uncanny look of mingled watchfulness and waggishness; at such times she appeared to be making up her mind whether to sneak off, to charge, or to dance! This is a common attitude, and one I have frequently observed when hunting. The effect is of a pretty direct line from nose to rump in contrast with the usual outline of the bear on all fours, where the shoulders are highest and the head and rump lowest. This attitude has something comical about it, and when seen assures the hunter that the animal is alert.

I watched this interesting family for about a week, and left them undisturbed until autumn. At that time bears were plentiful. In the same month and near the same place I saw eleven in one day, two black and nine silver tips, which I think was not far from the usual relative abundance of the two species in the Big Horn Mountains fifteen and twenty years ago.

I remember these incidents more distinctly than others that occurred to me. Unfortunately, in those days I thought, with many others, that game would continue in abundance much longer than proved to be the case, and so neglected to preserve many notes and specimens that to-day would be of very great interest.

J. C. Merrill.

THE BEAR'S DISPOSITION

My own experience with bears tends to make me lay special emphasis upon their variation in temper. There are savage and cowardly bears, just as there are big and little ones ; and sometimes these variations are very marked among bears of the same district, and at other times all the bears of one district will seem to have a common code of behavior which differs utterly from that of the bears of another district. Readers of Lewis and Clarke do not need to be reminded of the great difference they found in ferocity between the bears of the Upper Missouri and the bears of the Columbia River drainage system ; and those who have lived in the Upper Missouri country nowadays know how widely the bears that still remain have altered in character from what they were as recently as the middle of the century.

Bear Traits

This variability has been shown in the bears which I have stumbled upon at close quarters. On but one occasion was I ever regularly charged by a grizzly. To this animal I had given a mortal wound, and without any effort at retaliation he bolted into a thicket of what, in my hurry, I thought was laurel (it being composed in reality I suppose of thick-growing berry bushes). On my following him up and giving him a second wound, he charged very determinedly, taking two bullets without flinching. I just escaped the charge by jumping to one side, and he died almost immediately after striking at me as he rushed by. This bear charged with his mouth open, but made very little noise after the growl or roar with which he greeted my second bullet. I mention the fact of his having kept his mouth open, because one or two of my friends who have been charged have informed me that in their cases they particularly noticed that the bear charged with his mouth shut. Perhaps the fact that my bear was shot through the lungs may account for the difference, or it may simply be another example of individual variation.

On another occasion, in a windfall, I got up

within eight or ten feet of a grizzly, which simply bolted off, paying no heed to a hurried shot which I delivered as I poised unsteadily on the swaying top of an overthrown dead pine. On yet another occasion, when I roused a big bear from his sleep, he at the first moment seemed to pay little or no heed to me, and then turned toward me in a leisurely way, the only sign of hostility he betrayed being to ruffle up the hair on his shoulders and the back of his neck. I hit him square between the eyes, and he dropped like a pole-axed steer.

On another occasion I got up quite close to and mortally wounded a bear, which ran off without uttering a sound until it fell dead; but another of these grizzlies, which I shot from ambush, kept squalling and yelling every time I hit him, making a great rumpus. On one occasion one of my cow hands and myself were able to run down on foot a she grizzly bear and her cub, which had obtained a long start of us, simply because of the foolish conduct of the mother. The cub—or more properly the yearling, for it was a cub of the second year—ran on far ahead, and would have escaped if the old she had not continually stopped and sat up on her hind legs to look back at us. I think she did this partly from curiosity, but partly also from bad temper, for once or twice she grinned and roared at us. The upshot of it was that I got within range and put a bullet in the old she, who afterwards charged my companion and was killed, and we also got the yearling.

Another young grizzly which I killed dropped to the first bullet, which entered its stomach. It then let myself and my companion approach closely, looking up at us with alert curiosity, but making no effort to escape. It was really not crippled at all, but we thought from its actions that its back was broken, and my companion foolishly advanced to kill it with his pistol. The pistol, however, did not inflict a mortal wound, and the only effect was to make the young bear jump to its feet as if unhurt, and race off at full speed through the timber; for though not full-grown it was beyond cubhood, being probably about eighteen months old. By desperate running I succeeded in getting another shot, and more by luck than anything else knocked it over, this time permanently.

Black bear are not, under normal conditions, formidable brutes. They are not nearly so apt to charge as is a wild hog; but if they do charge and get home they will maul a man severely, and there are a number of instances on record in which they have killed men. Ordinarily, however, a black bear will not charge at all, though he may bluster a good deal. I once shot one very close up which made a most lamentable outcry, and seemed to lose its head, its efforts to escape resulting in its bouncing about among the trees with such heedless hurry that I was easily able to kill it. Another black bear, which I also shot at close quarters, came straight for my companions and myself, and almost ran over the white hunter who was with me. This bear made no sound whatever when I first hit it, and I do not think it was charging. I believe it was simply dazed, and by accident ran the wrong way, and so almost came into collision with us. However, when it found itself face to face with the white hunter, and only four or five feet away, it prepared for hostilities, and I think would have mauled him if I had not brained it with another bullet; for I was myself standing but six feet or so to one side of it.

Bear Traits

Ordinarily, however, my experience has been that bears were not flurried when I suddenly came upon them. They impressed me as if they were always keeping in mind the place toward which they wished to retreat in the event of danger, and for this place, which was invariably a piece of rough ground or dense timber, they made off with all possible speed, not seeming to lose their heads.

Frequently I have been able to watch bears for some time while myself unobserved. With other game I have very often done this even when within close range, not wishing to kill creatures needlessly, or without a good object; but with bears, my experience has been that chances to secure them come so seldom as to make it very distinctly worth while improving any that do come, and I have not spent much time watching any bear unless he was in a place where I could not get at him, or else was so close at hand that I was not afraid of his getting away. On one occasion the bear was hard at work digging up squirrel or gopher caches on the side of a pine-clad hill. He looked rather like a big badger when so engaged. On two other occasions the bear was working around a carcass preparatory to burying it. On these occasions I was very close, and it was extremely interesting to note the grotesque, half human movements, and giant, awkward strength of the great beast. He would twist the carcass around with the utmost ease, sometimes taking it in his teeth and dragging it, at other times grasping it in his forepaws and half lifting, half shoving it. Once the bear lost his grip and rolled over during the course of some movement, and this made him angry, and he struck the carcass a savage whack, just as a pettish child will strike a table against which it has knocked itself.

At another time I watched a black bear some distance off getting his breakfast under stumps and stones. He was very active, turning the stone or log over, and then thrusting his muzzle into the empty space to gobble up the small creatures below before they recovered from the surprise and the sudden inflow of light. From under one log he put up a chipmunk, and danced hither and thither with even more agility than awkwardness, slapping at the chipmunk with his paw while it zigzagged about, until finally he scooped it into his mouth.

Bear Traits

The Yellowstone Park now presents the best chance for observing the habits of bears that has ever been offered, for though they are wild in theory, yet in practice they have come to frequenting the hotels at dusk and after nightfall, as if they were half tame at least; and it is earnestly to be wished that some Boone and Crockett member who, unlike the present writer, does not belong to the laboring classes, would devote a month or two, or indeed a whole season, to the serious study of the life history of these bears. It would be time very well spent.

Theodore Roosevelt.

MODERN BEAR BAITING

Watching at a bait for game is intrinsically a much lower form of sport than stalking it. There is no opportunity for the prolonged generalship and shifting of tactics which lend to the stalking of mountain sheep, for instance, such fascinating interest. But to the modern hunter of bears in the West, especially in the autumn, there is practically no other method open. Instead of the easy-going bully of half a century ago, the hunter has now to find and outwit the most timid of nocturnal animals; a beast which clings to secluded recesses of wooded mountains, and can be tempted from its lair before nightfall only by the most alluring appeals to its appetite. In the course of nine trips to the Rocky Mountains, each of which was spent in a country where bears were fairly plentiful, hunting with the utmost care and patience of which I was capable, I have, without the aid of bait, seen them but twice.

In the northeastern provinces of Canada, on the other hand, where the bears in the season live mainly upon blueberries, and where forest shelter is always close by, I should say that though equally timid, they were much more given to feeding by daylight, and the hunter can often have the finest kind of fair stalking.

But in spite of its shortcomings, hunting with bait has features which make it a very absorbing sport. The careful watcher has unusual opportunities for studying the habits and actions of his game; though the tactics of his sport are simple, he will need all the patient, thoughtful strategy he can muster;

and finally, when his bear is the grizzly, there is the ever thrilling, if remote, chance of a charge. That chance seems far less remote when you are creeping down into some tangled ravine to meet your antagonist ravening at his food in the deepening twilight, than it would if you could stalk him in the open at midday and between meals.

I have never been actually charged by a bear. Twice my companion has thought he saw one feint or bluster at us. But on each occasion I was either busy with my rifle or attributed the motion to other causes. So I cannot speak from experience of the bear hunter's grand sensation—that of withstanding an assault.

On the other hand, I have had several rather unusual chances of watching a bear approach his bait. And I have also committed about every error of omission and commission by which the poor finite human being can betray his plans and purposes to the almost infinite sagacity of the creature he flatters himself he is going to outwit. Out of those countless blunders, theories of action have of necessity been hammered into me, some of which may possibly be useful to others. But to avoid coloring facts too much with theory it may be well to state the facts first.

In the summer of 1886 I spent my college vacation hunting with a Micmac Indian on the headwaters of a New Brunswick river. I had stalked and killed a lean old black bear on one of the small mountains that bordered the river near our camp, and so much of his carcass as we had not carried off for our larder, lay among the low blueberry bushes near the summit. About a week later we climbed up to it again, and found that it had been partly devoured by another bear. It was in August. Blueberries were ripe and marvelously plentiful. The new bear thus could not have been driven to cannibalism by those pangs of hunger by which some writers have thought it necessary to explain such an act.

It was about ten in the morning when we reached the carcass. Nicholas, the Indian, examined the carcass from above. I incautiously walked once around and below it, looking for the new bear's trail. We then retired to another spur of the mountain, whence at a distance of about 300 yards we could command the whole hillside on which the carcass lay. Our plan was to let the bear get at the bait, and then stalk it as we had stalked its predecessor. From the spot where the bait lay it would have been impossible, on account of the bushes, to see anything approaching.

The wind blew strongly up that hillside all day long; so strongly that we lay in comparative comfort in a place where the week before the black flies had made life a torment. At about four o'clock we saw a large bear coming up the hill, several hundred yards below the carcass. It came slowly but steadily, and without stopping, until it reached the exact spot where I had circled around the bait—a spot easily distinguishable by reason of an opening in the bushes. Then it stopped, and its nose went down to the ground.

"He smell your track," hissed a wrathful voice in my ear. The bear turned, and started slowly down; so slowly that, hoping it might stop or turn back, I refrained from taking the long shot which Nicholas was urging upon me. In a few yards, when it was well out of sight of the bait, though still in full view of us, its pace quickened to a trot, and then in a second it was plunging down

the hillside at a mad gallop. From first to
last it did not see or hear us, I am confident.
In the early morning we had seen from camp
a bear with a cub wandering over the same
hilltop, and as we dejectedly tramped down
that afternoon, we heard a cub squall in the
direction taken by the running bear; so I
have no doubt that our conqueror was a
female.

Four years afterward I was hunting, during
August and September, on the main range of
the Rockies between Steamboat Springs and
North Park, Colorado. Bears were still there
in good numbers, and our party of three—Mr.
A. P. Proctor and Dr. John Rogers were with
me—secured seven of them that summer,
counting all sizes and colors. One of my
baits lay in the center of an open meadow,
bordering a stream which ran sharply downward through a deep wooded valley leading
off the great range toward the low country on
the west. I had expected to watch it from a
spur of the forest on the side of the meadow;
but on coming to inspect it one morning I
found that it had been picked up by a bear on
the previous night, dragged across the meadow, and left on the edge of the woods at the

very point from which I had expected to watch. Closer examination showed that the bear, instead of coming up the valley from below, as I had expected, had entered and left the meadow close by the watching point, and that in coming I had already unwittingly crossed its trail.

With the experience in New Brunswick just mentioned sharply before me, I studied the situation. One thing was certain : I must be there before him, for he would be likely to bolt as soon as he crossed my trail. At the same time it was now impossible to wait for him at the watching point, for the wind would almost certainly give him my scent as he came down behind me through the woods. Out in the meadow there was no shelter near enough to shoot from. I finally reasoned that if he bolted directly back on his trail, I could scarcely hope for a good shot under any arrangement. But, as his trail led sharply up hill, there was a good chance that, instead of turning back, he might head for some dense cover down at one of the extremities of the meadow. I therefore chose a point near that cover, but so situated that I could witness the whole performance, and if he didn't bolt at all would have a fairly good chance to stalk him at the bait.

Shortly before sunset, my eye caught the glint of the sun's rays on something moving through the forest that clothed the side of the mountain above the meadow, and presently I made out a small black bear cantering down the trail I had crossed in the morning. When he reached my crossing, or its immediate neighborhood—a bush prevented me from seeing clearly—there was a few seconds' pause, and then he came scudding like a frightened cat away from the bait, and down the meadow toward the cover near which I was lying hidden.

So far the game had worked out according to calculations, and, with an inward smile of satisfaction, I sat up to take a smooth running shot about ninety yards away. Too sure! Just as my finger squeezed the trigger, he stopped dead short—perhaps having seen me rise—and after an ineffective attempt to check my rifle, my bullet ploughed well in front and clear of him. He was in the cover and out of sight before I could shoot again, and Proctor and Rogers, watching together in another valley, wondered, after the distant solitary report, whether I was being gobbled by an angry grizzly.

I dragged the bait back to its old position under a solitary dead spruce stub in the center of the meadow, and reinforced its attractions with some more choice dainties. Every night for several in succession, it was visited by a bear, but always during the darkness. I watched each evening until my sights went out, and was there again at daybreak, only to find a diminished bait and no bear. When you feed a creature for any length of time you are apt to acquire a sense of proprietorship in it, and I came quite to feel as if I had a brand on that bear. But the work was hard, and my patience began to run low. Finally, one afternoon I was delayed in starting for the bait until almost sunset. Though I hurried my horse down the three or four miles of rough mountain before me, the evening shadows gained so rapidly that when I finally leaped off to tie him a quarter of a mile above the bait, it was almost dark. Looking back from a hundred yards away, the pony was indistinguishable against the woods that bordered the meadow where I had tied him. In my tennis slippers I trotted silently down through the woods to a new watch point perhaps ninety yards from the old spruce stub. When I reached it, it was so dark that even out in the open the little bushes made mere black blotches against the lighter meadow grass. Under the old stub I could distinguish nothing. But, as I stood there in the silent crisp air there came the sound of something crunching and cracking at the old elk ribs. The rascal was stealing my bait again!

I slipped down off the watching point, stole around behind a low ridge of rock and ran down under cover of that to its further point, distant some thirty yards from the spruce stub. The bait lay on the other side of the stub from me now, and anything feeding was hidden by some bushes which grew around its base.

With my rifle at the ready I sprinted across this remaining distance. When almost there I stumbled over a dead stick in the long meadow grass and nearly fell. Instantly a large dark object leaped to the right from the bushes, and made off for the woods. As soon as I could straighten up I threw a bullet after it, much as one would throw a stone after a dog. At the shot a second black form, ap-

parently smaller, and, I think, a yearling or
two-year old black bear, raced out of the
bushes on the other side, and escaped without
a shot. Furious at losing both, I rushed into
the bushes to see if there were any more, and
a third, a cub, with a yelp of dismay, for I had
nearly trodden on him, scuttled up the spruce
stub. Walking around until I got him against
the light in the western sky, I am sorry to say
I shot and killed him. He was no larger than
a collie dog, and might much better have been
left to grow. Though she must have heard
him, and had the darkness to cover her approach, his faithless mother never returned,
but by her rapid flight helped to dispel in my
mind another historic illusion as to the invariable ferocity of she-bears.

Of course bears are not always so timid
about the scent of man as in the two cases I
have mentioned. I am inclined to think that
those were, perhaps, rather exceptional. Several times I have known grizzly bears, and
once a black—which in my experience has
appeared to be the more cautious species—to
come boldly to baits around which our scent
must have been much more in evidence than
at either of the times just mentioned. At the

same time the hunter is obliged to gauge his plans by the intelligence of the most, and not the least, wary. He must, therefore, be always able to inspect his bait, to see whether it has been touched, without leaving a trail which will be crossed by the bear when returning.

The greatest danger to success, however, is that your game will actually scent you while you are waiting for it. It is not always flattering to a gentleman's feelings to observe the rapidity with which a beast, which has only been pleased and attracted by the overpowering stench of the carcass beside you, will be put to headlong flight by the faintest whiff of you. But one can count with the utmost positiveness on that result.

The problem of avoiding this is complicated by two uncertainties—that of the direction from which the bear will come, and that of the direction from which the wind will blow at the time when he comes. So far as possible these two uncertainties must be eliminated beforehand. The first must be carefully studied out from the facts of each case—such as the direction of the nearest dense cover and water, and the general lay of the land. By placing one's bait rather high up in a mountainous country you can usually force your bear to approach from below, and you can generally count on his following the cover afforded by ravines and watercourses.

As regards the wind, one must constantly bear in mind the fact, which every hunter in a hilly or mountainous country must have noticed, namely, that in the absence of a very strong prevailing wind, the air regularly draws up a valley or gulch during the daytime only to chop around and draw down directly the sun has set. As your watching period must cover the time both just before and after sunset, your watch point must be so arranged that the bear will not get your scent with the wind in either of those directions. Add to this changeable nature of the breeze, the well-known fact that a wary bear will usually take a quiet circle through the woods all around the bait before going to it, and the complex elements of the problem become apparent.

To solve it, some people recommend watching from a tree. This probably would be effective in removing your scent, but it would also go far toward removing the last vestige of manliness from the sport, and though I have sometimes compromised on a steep slope or rock, I confess I could never quite go a tree.

There is another way, though, of avoiding the difficulty, which, I think, rather adds to than diminishes the excitement and interest of bait-hunting. That is to let the bear satisfy his suspicions, and get actually at the bait before you make your approach. To do this successfully, one should choose, if possible, two posts of vantage, one at a comparatively long distance—two or three hundred yards— from the bait, to watch from, and the other forty or fifty yards away, to shoot from. These should, of course, be carefully chosen with a view to the lay of the land and the bear's probable approach, and a path between them should then be carefully selected, by which the hunter can steal down to the shooting point as soon as he sees from the watching point that the bear has begun his meal. Then, creeping down on his quarry, one can bring to use all the caution of the still-hunter, and even much of the stalker's skill, while at the final shot he meets his adversary on a fair field.

I recall a hunt when I tried this arrangement, however, which will serve to show the

Bear Traits

necessity of care In the choice of position, for other reasons than the shyness of the bears. It is not a pleasant hunt for me to recall, for it contained the best and most misused opportunity I ever had.

I was camping in northwestern Montana, in a country whose magnificent mountains and glaciers had for three years caused me to discard bear-hunting for the superior pleasures of mountaineering. My wife and I were alone, except for our man Fox and his eighteen-year-old boy. Toward the end of our trip an Indian friend, who had joined us for a few days' visit, rather unnecessarily killed a fine old mountain goat. The meat was, of course, rank and uneatable, and as we had seen bear signs five or six miles down the valley, at the head of which we were camped, in order not to waste it, I asked Fox to pack the carcass down there, and arrange a bear bait. He had never hunted bears with bait, but I explained to him the method I have just described, and asked him if possible to arrange the bait so as to conform to it. He was gone all day, and on his return in the evening said that he had found a place where he was certain the bait would be visited, but that he was not quite satisfied with the shooting and watch points. He is such an habitually modest man that I did not give this remark full weight at the time.

The next day we moved our camp some six miles down the valley, so as to be a little nearer the bait, and a little further from the great glacier at the valley's head, whose propensity for collecting storms was getting to be a little monotonous. After camp had been pitched, I decided to go over with Fox to the bait, mainly because Fox was anxious to have me see whether it had been properly arranged. As he had left it only the day before, and had tramped all over the place where it was with two horses, we had no idea that it had yet been visited.

It had been rather a bad day for me. While coming down the valley my scatterbrained pony, in trying to clear a windfall had thrown himself heavily with me underneath, and, though I luckily escaped injury, the shock had given me a racking headache. So I followed Fox rather mechanically as he threaded his way through the quaking aspens that clothed the mountain side on which the bait lay. A fierce wind was blowing down the valley, and, while the sky was clear overhead, it dashed a fine horizontal spray into our faces from the storm that still overhung the great glacier seven or eight miles distant. The bait was further than we had counted, and when Fox finally slid from his horse, the sun had already dropped into the cloudbank at the valley's head. Picketing the ponies, we ran down to an open knoll, which Fox said was the watch point. From its foot a dry brook-bed ran down through a sparse half-burnt second growth of woods to a little meadow, which could only be partly seen, some three hundred yards away. "The bait lies in that meadow," said Fox, "near that large bush."

I studied it carefully through my field glass. The light in the meadow was already rather dim, and the bushes looked gray, but I could see nothing that looked like a bear. I could not, however, even clearly distinguish the bait. Fox took the glass. "There's nothing there," he said. "Let's go down, and see how you fastened it, anyway," I proposed. A goat's carcass being so small, Fox had tied it to a log to prevent it from being dragged bodily away.

Fox led the way down the dry brook-bed. It was five or six feet deep, and made capital cover for one's approach. Finally he stopped, and motioned to me to go ahead. "The watch point is just around that bend," he whispered. I stepped around it, and there the brook-bed debouched into the meadow. Just at its mouth was a small pile of brush, arranged by Fox as a cover. I looked over it, and saw, about fifty yards away, a grizzly bear, standing quartering toward me and my left, with his forefeet resting on something hidden in the bushes below it—apparently the bait. The meadow, which had seemed to be grassy from above, now showed itself waist-high with sarvice berry bushes. The chamber of my rifle was still unloaded, and I threw a shell into it; Fox had no gun. The front white Lyman bead came clearly against the bear's left shoulder, and I pulled. She went down with a muffled roar, and lay out of sight in the bushes, still roaring and groaning.

Instantly another large bear rose on its hind feet from behind a bush in the center of the meadow, while a third rushed into it from the woods on the right. To my startled imagination the meadow seemed to be sprouting with grizzlies. The fellow in the center, to judge from his tracks, must have stood over six feet high; he looked about ten. It was already too dusky to see clearly the rear Lyman sight. I had noticed that on my first shot; but I threw a bullet at this second bear without looking through my sights at all—just as you would shoot at a flying quail. And as both bears rushed off into the woods on the left together, I pumped two more shots after them, like the veriest tenderfoot.

Then, just as they disappeared, I noticed that the wounded bear was on its feet, and plunging heavily off, with its shoulder swinging loose, somewhat further down the meadow than where the others had gone. I remember the sickening thought came over me—"I shall lose them all"—and pulling myself somewhat together, I made a good shot at her just as she reached the woods. She seemed to fall in a heap at the edge of some willows. Fox, standing beside me, said: "You've got that one all right."

Shoving some more cartridges into my magazine as I ran, I hurried into the woods after the other two bears, passing just above, and where I could hear but not see the wounded bear growling and thrashing in the thick willows. I ran over the top of the little hill over which they had gone, and almost ran into them, standing there together among the sparse "quaken ash." One rose to its hind-legs, and I missed it again—how, even without sights, I don't know; I could almost have poked it with my gun. They wheeled, and raced into the bushes behind them, and, seeing that I had missed, I went back to Fox to look for the wounded bear.

She was not where she had fallen, and her noise had stopped. It was already quite dark under the willow bushes. We circled closely all around them, peering beneath. They were only a small patch lying on the edge of the woods, and we could see everything except the very center, which could only be reached on hands and knees. We decided to leave that part till morning. Then, after looking also through the surrounding woods, I sent Fox back for the horses, and watched beside the bushes for the twenty minutes or so that he was gone. Nothing more stirred, and we rode back to camp.

It rained hard all night, and it was still raining heavily when, long before daylight, we returned with young Fox to the bait. There is no need of dwelling on the disappointment of that morning. There was no bear under the bushes, and whatever blood she had left on her trail had long since been washed away. We quartered over the surrounding woods, foot by foot, for five or six hours. Then I sent the men home, and continued it till afternoon. After I had got something to eat and some dry clothes, I found it impossible to stay in camp, and decided to watch the bait again that evening.

Just before sunset I struck into the dry brook-bed below the watch point, and followed it carefully down to the bend. Looking around it, I again saw two grizzlies with their heads down at the goat's carcass—evidently the same two bears that had escaped the night before. Setting my teeth, I determined to take no more chances with a .45-90 at a bear's body, but to rest my rifle over the brush, and make a steady shot for the head. The brush pile was about ten feet away. Dropping on hands and knees I crawled to it, and then cautiously rose up. They could not have seen me, but some whirl of air had evidently given them my scent, for they were both moving across the meadow toward the place where they had left it before. One was running steadily, but the other half stopped at intervals to rear and take a quick look over the bushes in my direction.

I stood up for a running shot, and as he reared the second time, I drove my bullet at his great chest with all the steadiness the quick shot would allow. With a snarl like that of a fighting dog, he went over backward. He was on his feet again so quickly that it looked to me as if he had turned a back somersault, and racing after his companion, caught him up within forty yards, in his haste seeming almost to run over him. I sighted at him again through the trees, but held a shade too long, and as I pulled saw him sink below the hilltop, and felt I had shot over. I followed a good blood trail till dark; and on the next morning, with Fox, followed it for nearly two miles, when we lost it on some open ground.

Out of those two evenings I have drawn several lessons—most of them derogatory to myself, and to the experience which I thought ten seasons of big game hunting had left in me. But there were also some features for which personal failings did not entirely account. The second bear was probably hit too high. I did not then realize how high a

bear's head and neck tower when he stands
erect, and how proportionately low his heart
and lungs sink down. Watch one in Central
Park some time and see. I feel sure the first
bear did not live long after the shot, and even
as it was, with a good dog we should undoubtedly have recovered her. But good bear dogs
are scarce, and dog or no dog, either of those
bears could have eaten me up, had it so
chosen. Moreover, I was sufficiently acquainted with my own power, to know that I could
not count regularly on doing better shooting
than I had done in my first shot at the first
bear.

I had used the .45-90 Winchester for five
years, and was fully sensible of its accuracy,
flatness, and other good features. But I decided to discard it for bait hunting. Every
one who has depended on its solid hardened
bullet has seen game go good distances even
when fatally hit, and the subject of its merits
and demerits, as compared with a hollow point
or soft lead bullet, has been so thoroughly
thrashed out of late that it is superfluous now
to go through it.

Suffice to say, that I decided in future to
use a special gun for bait shooting, of which

one shot should be warranted to be effective. This, however, was before smokeless powder, with its resultant high velocity, had come into sporting use, and I had to depend upon black powder. The following winter the Winchester Company made me up a gun which, I think, will fulfill the conditions above given. It is a single shot .577-caliber rifle, shooting 167 grains of powder, and a 600-grain bullet, with a small hollow in the point. Even after the point breaks off and scatters there is over 400 grains of solid butt left—more than sufficient to break any bone.

I have only shot it at one animal as yet. This was a rather small bear, of the kind known as the cinnamon in many parts of the Northwest, but short-clawed, and really a variety of black. He was standing on all four legs, facing me, some fifty yards away, with his head down at the bait. At the shot he fell forward, and never moved. The bullet entered the heavy muscles of the neck, and passed backward and downward through the thorax. After entering, its front end broke up, and left a track through which I could pass my unclenched hand. Fox, who was there, looked at the hole, and said solemnly:

Bear Traits

"If you had only had that gun last fall!" The foregoing cases, taken as examples, show how dangerous it is to generalize too much about the conduct of bears at a bait. Individual bears vary in their character, just as human beings do. And even the same bear may act very differently at different times. I remember one bear stealing up so quietly, that two of us, listening with all our ears, never heard him until he reached the bait. And the next night, after having been shot at and well scared, he came back over the same course, and made noise enough to rouse the dead.

So much do individuals vary, that it is quite hard to recognize regular characteristic differences between even the grizzly and the black. The grizzlies that I have seen seemed to be bolder, and to come earlier to bait, than their black cousins in the West; but friends have told me of cases where an old grizzly was as shy and cautious as a fox. In the East, as I said before, I have several times seen black bears feeding at midday. In nearly every case that I have seen, the grizzly, too, tried to bury or cache his bait. Sometimes this attempt was very perfunctory—merely a few handfuls of grass or earth scratched over it; but I do not remember a black bear ever doing even so much as that.

I should say, also, that the two species differed usually as well in their behavior under fire. I have seen eight grizzlies and six black bears shot. Two of the former and one of the latter were instantaneously killed. Of the remainder, every one of the grizzlies bellowed and roared tremendously when hit, while every one of the blacks, except the cub in the spruce stub above mentioned, took his punishment in perfect silence. I have seen but one bear of any kind, however, keep its feet when struck. Unlike an elk, which rarely even flinches, a bear will nearly always throw itself headlong, clawing or biting at the wound. The solitary exception that I remember was a black bear in New Brunswick. Though fatally hit, she only flinched slightly, and withdrew into the bushes from which she had just appeared.

In this sensitiveness to wounds, the bear seems to resemble the cat tribe. The only one that I have ever watched for any length of time, close by, also reminded me somewhat of a cat in his motions and behavior. It was

Bear Traits

the small "cinnamon" above mentioned, and as he approached the bait I watched him for at least ten minutes, within a distance of a hundred yards. He was extremely nervous, walking very slowly, and stopping every few minutes to look and listen. At these times he would raise his head, and look about in all directions. Something startled him, and he dashed sideways half-way up a leaning tree-trunk, for all the world like a scared cat. Then he crept down, circled slowly around out of sight below the bait, and I did not see him until his head quietly pushed through the wlllows, near which the bait lay. There he stopped, with his long nose screwed up in a savory anticipation, and it was a full minute before he finally stepped out of the bushes, walked across the remaining ten feet, and began his meal.

Henry L. Stimson.

The Adirondack Deer Law

A Convention to revise and amend the Constitution of the State of New York was held at the City of Albany in the summer of 1894. Among the changes proposed by the Convention was the addition of the following words, as Section 7 of Article VII. of the Constitution:

"The lands of the State, now owned or hereafter acquired, constituting the Forest Preserve as now fixed by law, shall be forever kept as wild forest lands. They shall not be leased, sold or exchanged, or taken by any corporation, public or private, nor shall the timber be sold, removed or destroyed."

At the election in the autumn of the same year the new Constitution was approved and ratified by a popular vote, and on the 1st day of January, 1895, it went into effect. This action by the people through their delegates, and at the polls, made plain the fact that the

importance of preserving the great North
Woods was clearly recognized. These forests
affect the climate of the State, increase its
water supply, contain many valuable health
resorts, and afford an ideal range of territory
for the protection and preservation of deer—
the only kind of large game now remaining
in the State of New York. As is well known,
the species which is found in the Adirondack
Woods is variously designated as the Virginia
deer, red deer, common deer, and white-tailed
deer; and, as Caton says in his "Deer and Antelope of America," has been found in every
State and Territory of the United States, as
well as in Canada, British Columbia and
Mexico. Col. William F. Fox, Superintendent
of Forests, in the State of New York, says, in
a recent most valuable report, that in the
Southern States "the species is inferior in
size, being fully one-third smaller than the
northern deer. The Adirondack deer, while
not exhibiting, perhaps, the very largest and
finest type, will compare favorably with those
of Maine and Michigan, where the species is
seen at its best. In the Adirondack region
it attains a maximum weight of about 350
pounds. The largest recorded size—a buck,

killed in Warren County—showed a height of 4 feet 3 inches over the withers, with a length from nose to tip of tail of 9 feet 7 inches."

For every reason it is important to give proper protection to these animals, whose grace and beauty make them of interest to all who visit the woods, and whose pursuit in fair chase gives keen pleasure to the sportsman.

Many years ago deer were shot when they came to the salt licks; but a wise law long since prohibited this, as well as the use of traps. Two objectionable methods of killing deer were, however, still permitted by law, and generally practiced throughout the Adirondacks when the new Constitution went into effect. One was jacking, and the other was driving the deer with hounds to deep water, and shooting them while swimming. In jacking, the hunter is paddled silently along the edge of a lake, with a bright light in the bow of the boat or fastened to his hat; a deer, fascinated by the light, stands watching it, until a load of buckshot is fired in the direction of the shining eyes of the deer, which, as a rule, are the only parts of the animal which can be distinguished. Reliable authorities have estimated, that only one in four of the deer thus killed is secured, the others running to some distant or secluded spot before lying down to die of their wounds, and that four-fifths of those secured are nursing does, whose un-weaned fawns are left to die of starvation. Little can be said in defense of this method of hunting.

The objection to driving deer to deep water is that their escape is practically impossible, as a man in a boat can row faster than any deer can swim. Even a child can thus be rowed around the swimming animal, and can shoot at him until a lucky shot kills. One of the best guides in the Adirondacks told me that he had seen a man fire thirty-two shots at a swimming deer before the clumsy butchery ended.

The lovers of fair sport were encouraged by the increased interest in our forests, on the part of the people, as evidenced by the adoption of the section of the new Constitution already quoted, to hope for legislation which would wisely protect the deer. Their contention rested upon two fundamental propositions: First, that the preservation of deer in our State was so desirable, that they should be protected from such methods of slaughter

267

as might result either in their extermination
or migration ; and, second, that, entirely inde-
pendent of whether deer were increasing or
diminishing in numbers, they should be protected from cruel or unsportsmanlike methods
of killing. That jacking is cruel and unsportsmanlike few would deny, and that killing deer
in deep water would hasten their extermination
is the firm belief of many who are well qualified to form an accurate judgment. For these
reasons, both in the interest of sport, and for
the better protection of the deer, the most
earnest efforts were made in the years 1895,
1896, and 1897 to secure the enactment of
laws prohibiting jacking and hounding. During this time I was a member of the Legislature, so that, in telling of what was attempted,
and what was accomplished, I can say, in the
words of the narrator of another story :

> . . . *quæque ipse* . . . *vidi*
> *et quorum pars* . . . *fui.*

When the session of 1895 opened, the general law permitted the killing of deer from the
15th of August to the 1st of November ;
hounding was permitted from September 10th
to October 10th, and there was no prohibition
against jacking. Special laws regulated deer

hunting on Long Island, and in the five counties of St. Lawrence, Delaware, Greene, Ulster, and Sullivan, in some of which hounding was prohibited. Mr. W. W. Niles, Jr., a member of Assembly from New York City, introduced a bill prohibiting absolutely both jacking and hounding, but, notwithstanding the able and earnest work of Mr. Niles and others, the proposed law failed of passage.

During this year the " Fisheries, Game and Forest Law " was enacted, and, in accordance with one of its provisions, the Governor appointed the "Fisheries, Game and Forest Commission," which has from the outset done admirable work for the great interests which are under its supervision.

Under the direction of a Committee of the Senate, a revision of the Game Laws was prepared, but it was not submitted to the Legislature until the concluding days of the session. The only change which was proposed in the law concerning deer, was the substitution of the 16th for the 15th of August as the opening day of the season, and with this unimportant change of one day as a result of the year's work on the deer laws, the Legislature adjourned.

As set forth in its Constitution, one of the objects of the Boone and Crockett Club is "To work for the preservation of the large game of this country, and, so far as possible, to further legislation for that purpose." It is needless to say that during all this time the members of the club, and other sportsmen throughout the State, were earnestly interested in the question thus presented to the Legislature. Now and then some well-known woodsman would urge the importance of shortening the season, leaving the methods of killing unchanged, but almost invariably it would be found that he never hunted with a jack-light, or killed a deer when swimming. A few good sportsmen who used dogs to drive their deer to runways, but who never shot them in deep water, opposed the prohibition of hounding, and, in order to meet the case of those who thus hunted with hounds, it was suggested that a law be passed prohibiting the killing of deer in deep water. The impossibility of enforcing such a law was speedily recognized by all, and its advocates soon abandoned it.

It is, I think, no exaggeration to say that the best sportsmen in the State, with here and there an exception, favored the absolute

prohibition of both jacking and hounding.
Mr. Madison Grant, whose devotion to all
that concerns the best interests of sport is
well known, was tireless in submitting to com-
mittees and members of the Legislature facts
and arguments. Mr. George Bird Grinnell,
well qualified to speak authoritatively on all
hunting questions, whose personal experiences
with big game go back to the time when
myriads of buffalo wandered over the Western
prairies, lent to the proposed legislation the
strength of his favorable endorsement. Mr.
Robert C. Alexander, the President of the
Adirondack League Club, both personally and
through the columns of the *Mail and Express*,
gave to those who were contending for the
laws his forceful and helpful influence. In
1896, the Hon. George R. Malby, of St. Lawrence County, introduced in the Senate bills
prohibiting entirely hounding and jacking,
which he ably advocated and passed through
the Senate.

Similar bills were introduced in the Assembly. They were earnestly championed by the
Hon. Martin Van Buren Ives, of St. Lawrence
County, and others. The Fisheries, Game
and Forest Commission prepared a report,

showing that 5,000 deer were killed in the
Adirondacks during 1895, and they officially
expressed the opinion that both jacking and
hounding should be prohibited; but despite
such endorsement, and the most strenuous
efforts of the friends of the bills, they failed to
pass. Some of the arguments used against
the measures were, that the proposed legislation was in the interest of a few rich men who
owned large preserves; that it would injure
the business of the guides and the hotels; and
that the deer, under the existing law, were increasing so rapidly that there was not food
enough for them in winter, so that many
starved to death. With such statements, members from certain Adirondack counties made
an earnest personal appeal against the bills,
and it was found that it would be impossible
to secure their passage.

A compromise measure was, therefore,
framed, which left the open season unchanged,
but prohibited hounding and jacking, except
between the 1st and 15th days of October;
and this measure, notwithstanding a most determined opposition, was passed, and received
the Governor's signature.

In the autumn of 1895 I was a candidate

for re-election to the Legislature. The entire
country was stirred by the financial questions
at issue, and there was an uninterrupted series
of public meetings in central New York, as
elsewhere, at which these questions were discussed. During the six weeks preceding the
election I spoke almost every evening, but I
was exceedingly desirous of making a visit to
the woods, for the purpose of finding out the
sentiment of the guides and hotel-keepers regarding jacking and hounding, and incidentally of doing a little still-hunting. Arranging
so that there were no engagements to speak
from one Saturday until the following Thursday, and leaving home on Saturday, I found
myself Sunday morning in the woods. A long
tramp that day proved conclusively that the
law which prohibited hunting on Sunday was
openly and persistently violated. I came
across parties who were watching on runways
for the deer that might be driven in by their
hounds, and was nearly fired at by one eager
sportsman, who was ready to shoot at any
object he saw moving through the undergrowth. Monday morning I made an early
start, and spent the day in the woods searching for game.

Trail and Camp-Fire

I think it was Sir William Thompson who said, that if he were offered his choice between the possession of knowledge and its pursuit, he would unhesitatingly choose the pursuit. I must admit that I am somewhat of that philosopher's mind in regard to game, for the pleasure of a day's hunting has never been dependent upon the quantity of game bagged. When the country through which one hunts is beautiful the days have an added pleasure.

Many years ago I spent some time among the Harz Mountains in Germany, hunting in the preserves of the Duke of Brunswick. The richness in legend and fable, and the wild beauty of that region, made it a delight, even when no shot was fired, to roam over mountain or through valley, trying to find game in the daytime, or watching for wild boars by moonlight. So, in our own North Woods, it is not necessary even to see a deer, in order to lie down contentedly to dreamless sleep on the balsam boughs. Nature herself repays all the labor of forcing a way through the tangled underbrush, struggling through swamp, or climbing rocky hillsides. But, were the country without an attractive feature, the true sportsman would find in the chase itself ample reward for all his labors, and if his efforts to come upon a deer by still-hunting are crowned with success, he may reasonably feel the most intense satisfaction.

In the deer the sense of smell and hearing are remarkably developed. A tree may fall, making the mountain side re-echo as it crashes to the ground, and the deer is undisturbed; but the careless footstep which breaks a twig or snaps a branch puts him instantly on guard against the approaching enemy, and if the hunter moves as noiselessly as the falling snow, he is doomed to failure if he approaches the deer down the wind. Sometimes the hunter will come upon a deer browsing, without having previously tracked it, and his eyesight must be keen to distinguish the game among the trees before it is alarmed and disappears. When the track is followed, it is well to do as Mr. Barringer, in his interesting article, "Dog Sledging in the North," in the "Book of the Boone and Crockett Club," says the Indians do in following moose—leave the track continually in semicircles down wind.

All day Monday I traveled up hill and down, without seeing track or trace of deer, but with much pleasurable discourse with the guide who accompanied me. Tuesday I went further north, and covered many miles, in company with a splendid specimen of the Adirondack guide and woodsman. We found fresh tracks, and once we saw three deer—a buck and two does—but not near enough to justify shooting. Both days the woods were very dry, but Tuesday night it rained, and Wednesday morning, in a drizzling fall of mist, I started out again. At about ten o'clock I saw, through the dense foliage of a fallen tree, the form of a moving deer. Stopping instantly, I waited, and in a few seconds saw the head and neck exposed to plain view, at a distance of about sixty yards. A fortunate shot broke the vertebra, and the deer died instantly.

Among the guides and hotel-keepers whom I met, there was a growing sentiment in favor of the entire prohibition of hounding and jacking. The limit of two weeks' time made it a profitless expense to keep dogs for eleven and a half months, when they could only be used for two weeks.

So many visitors now come to the Adirondacks, that the conditions are very different from those which prevailed a decade ago, and

many men who had been most devoted to
hounding, were forced to admit that if the
deer are to be preserved, they must be protected from a form of hunting which makes
their death inevitable when they get into the
water. The unsportsmanlike method of shooting the swimming deer from a boat was generally deprecated.

Greatly encouraged by what I had learned,
I went back to the Legislature, hopeful that
during the session of 1897 satisfactory legislation could be secured, and this proved to be
the case. The contest was renewed with increased energy. Notwithstanding the force
of fact and argument, it was still impossible to
pass a law prohibiting absolutely these two
methods of hunting; but a compromise law
was enacted, by which they were prohibited
for five years.

Any one who kills deer must recognize that
the contest at best is an unequal one. The
man with a rifle is at such a great advantage
that there is comparatively little to be proud
of in killing a deer under any circumstances.
But when one is compelled to match his physical endurance, his woodcraft, and his skill as
a hunter, against the deer's natural instinct,

which enables it to detect, with such wonderful keenness of smell or hearing, the presence of a man, he can feel that he has at least secured his game in a way that can fairly be called sportsmanlike.

Let us hope that when five years have passed, no one will be found to oppose the passage of a law which will extend indefinitely the prohibition against hunting deer with jacklights, and shooting them when swimming in deep water.

Wm. Cary Sanger.

A Newfoundland Caribou Hunt

There is that about the island of Newfoundland which suggests caribou. The rugged ground breaks in flinty billows everywhere, yet leaves now and again a spot of oily calm, a level reach of yellow barren. The woodlands are evergreens that picture snows and wintry winds even in golden summer days; and everywhere grow tangles of wiry vines and undergrowth, conquered here and there by the level, bushy tops of berry plants. And beneath all is a soft carpet of gray moss, ankle-deep and moist, which the caribou so dearly love—moss, which to them is a luxury in summer, a necessity in winter, a feast always. And then there are a myriad lakes, great and small, lapping incessantly in vain endeavor to smooth their soft beaches of the countless cloven tracks, that vanish in the daylight only to form again like mushrooms in the dark, as countless as before.

We traveled to Grand Pond by rail and water, and there our outfit met us, and we branched forth from civilization into the wilderness.

It required three days' hard rowing to reach the Upper Birchy Pond. Our flotilla consisted of two eighteen-foot dories, railroaded for us from Bay of Islands, and a light Peterborough canoe, kindly loaned by young Mr. Reed. My father chose this latter for his flagship, and I paddled him, while into the two transports were loaded our complete outfit, together with our old Rocky Mountain guide, Mr. Keller, two hunters, three packers, the cook, and a Newfoundland puppy of mastodontic proportions.

I have never seen more ideal watercourses for trout or salmon, and despite the lateness of the season we had no difficulty in supplying the pan with an abundance of both. Only the smaller salmon took the fly; but we knew the big fellows lurked beneath our keels, for frequently, from some swirling pool at the foot of a rapid, one would shoot a clear two feet into the air, and fall gleaming back again with resounding slap. Then we would hungrily watch the circle ripples run apart and lap on either bank, and a yearning would fill our hearts.

A Newfoundland Caribou Hunt

Perhaps we would halt the march, and cast a tempting fly a dozen times or more. But soon this became a mere matter of form, for the big fish would not accept any challenge. They had retired from the ring till the next season, and they kept their resolution scrupulously.

Newfoundland geographers have odd ways. Amongst others they call lakes, miles broad and long, ponds. Hence, when Sir William informed us we should have to traverse a half dozen or so "ponds" to reach the Upper Birchy Pond, we were expectant of a few hours' paddling at most. Imagine our surprise and mild consternation when, at the end of the first day's hard labor, we had traversed but two of these so-called ponds. Then there were smaller lakes not accounted for at all, but classed by these generous explorers as widenings in the river. Some of these even required an hour to cross. But the work was pleasant, with the constant expectation of a shot at caribou and the excitement of the rapids, and I, for one, was not sorry to see our jaunt lengthening into a journey.

On the second day, as we were crossing Sandy Pond, one of the guides, William

Beaton, sighted a bull caribou a mile away upon the beach. Instantly the march stopped, and our glasses were leveled.

As I had never shot a caribou, I was appointed a committee of one to bring him into camp. I demurred, but my father insisted; so he climbed into the dory, and William into the canoe, I meanwhile unbuckling my .45-70 Winchester, and taking my seat in the bow. Then, with a parting "good-luck," and bit of advice not to shoot from too far off, we were away, and as we left the motionless flotilla I heard my father say: "That's all right; I'll wager the boy gets him." And I trembled for myself. Suppose I should miss in plain sight of all!

William bore a friendly rivalry to Keller, the Rocky Mountain man, and exerted himself to the utmost. The canoe was rapidly and silently stealing toward a wooded point that projected into the lake, some three hundred yards to windward of our quarry, and I, watching through my glasses, saw the bull grow and grow, until he loomed a monster indeed. Soon I could even count the larger points upon his antlers, and I saw he had a splendid head.

A Newfoundland Caribou Hunt

He was walking leisurely back and forth, feeding from some bushes overhanging the golden beach. Then a noise from the watching dories met his ears. Calmly he walked to the water's edged and gazed at them. I feared he would sight us, but he did not, and the low canoe crept on unseen. Then, satisfied that the dories were harmless, the regal fellow returned up the beach, showed his back to the lake, and deliberately lay down. How my heart exulted!

Gliding swiftly, we passed behind the point, and lost sight of our noble quarry. I judged that I should have to shoot about two hundred yards, and so gauged my Lyman sight. With the least possible noise our canoe grated upon the round stones of the beach, and I stepped cautiously into the ankle-deep water, and held the gunwale while William got out. In doing so he accidentally struck his paddle against the stern. My heart stood still. We listened apprehensively, but no sound came from across the point; all was silent as the grave. Then we began to walk swiftly up the shore, William leading. Fifty steps and we rounded the point, stooping low.

Yes, there lay the bull, head down, back to

us, and to all appearances asleep. In full sight we crept forward. A fallen balsam stretched across the beach, a dozen yards ahead, and I resolved to shoot from there. The metallic click! click! of the hob-nails in my boots against the stones warned me to approach no nearer.

I set my sight for 175 yards, and, leaning forward, rested my rifle across the fallen balsam. Instantly it plunged and reared like a gun-shy horse. Several dry branches cracked, and to my dismay I saw the bull spring up and face us, quartering.

I tried to shoot above the bobbing tree, but it was too high. Stooping, I sought another aim, but I was badly cramped, and the whipping of the branches before my eyes bothered me. Nevertheless, I caught the white of a shoulder through my sights, and fired.

The caribou moved one step forward, and a branch snipped from a bush just over his back. I knew I had shot too high. Lowering my rifle I depressed the sight to 150 yards. Then I dropped flat on my stomach, and while the bull still stood motionless, unable to locate the seat of danger, I drew a careful bead for his shoulder, well back, and fired again.

A Newfoundland Caribou Hunt

At the crack he plunged forward and ran, side on, down the beach. Pumping the lever, I swung ahead of him, waited, saw his head enter my sight, then his shoulder, and fired again. Instantly he pitched headlong, and lay motionless at the water's edge.

A sound came over the lake—the fall and sweep of oars. The butchers were coming. My part was done.

I arose and started down the beach. I think my contentment was perfect. I patted my Winchester lovingly.

"Those are nice cartridges," I said.

William smiled most affably.

"That's a good gun," he remarked. "You didn't need your third shot."

And, smiling amiably together, we continued our walk.

At the spot where the bull had stood and received my first and second salutes, we halted.

The sand was trampled and crushed into a regular caribou camp. Evidently the old fellow had been living there many days, waiting, no doubt, for his cows to swim across the lake to him.

We saw where my first shot had nipped the

bush ; and, yes, we saw clear evidence of my second. A drift of hair upon the sand and a shot streak of blood. William was right about my third shot.

Then we walked to the fallen monarch. He was quite dead.

My second bullet had passed an inch behind my third through the very center of his shoulder. Both shots were mortal. He was a magnificent specimen, white, with snowy neck of shaggy hair, and splendid antlers. The brow plows were exceptionally fine. One was enormous, measuring 18½ inches in breadth, with twelve points upon it. The other was a single, long, sword-like point. He had thirty-six points, all well defined. He was a very old stag, and his horns were the color of a black-tail deer's, from being cleaned on burnt tree trunks. They had an unusual spread and beam.

"You'll kill a hundred and not get a better head," said William.

After the caribou was dressed, the official distance of my shots, 163 and 197 yards, was ascertained, and we again embarked.

We experienced some considerable difficulty in finding the outlet, or rather inlet, in the upper end of this Sandy Pond water, and for two hours we paddled back and forth hunting it. While doing so a band of caribou were sighted upon the beach a mile away, and my father and William stalked them in the canoe while we watched. But the three bulls of the band all proved too small, and, after chasing them down the shore to see them run, the hunters returned empty-handed.

Then we found the stream we sought, and began to ascend it. Its mouth had formed a delta into the lake, and the channel wound in and out and about in a most fearful and wonderful fashion, that kept us guessing, and more over board, pushing and shoving, than in board. But an hour's toiling brought us safely through and well into the main stream, and a more beautiful stretch of water I have never seen.

Deep and purple black it wound between banks that overhung our heads with a wreath of verdure, flamed scarlet here and there by a species of wild cranberry. It was an ideal trout stream, and at the foot of the rapids we camped beside that night we caught as many of the speckled aristocrats as we desired and as the pan demanded.

The next morning we were off early, and as

I recall that third day now it seems an endless
journey through lakes that began every mile
and never ended. The truth is that each dory
was rowed by four strong men, and I paddled
that canoe alone, and a strong dead wind
sprang up and added to my toil.

But about four in the afternoon the wind
increased so greatly and the waves swelled to
such dimensions that it was no longer possible
to proceed with any degree of safety in the
canoe, and so we shifted to the dories and
towed our little craft behind. It was just
after this that I spied a young bull caribou
swimming directly toward us across the lake,
narrowed to a few hundred yards at this
point.

We remained motionless as he swam up,
but we did not stop talking. On he came,
swimming strong and turning his head this
way and that to stare with his great eyes at
our strange selves. Now and again a wave,
larger than its fellows, would break upon his
nose. Then, with a grunt of disapproval, the
bull would raise himself with furious strokes
half out of the water and shake his head
violently. Soon he had approached within a
hundred yards of us. Then he decided he

would give us a wider berth, and sheered off a few points, making for the land a couple of hundred yards above us. At once the idea of catching the youngster occurred to us, and with a wild yell the chase began.

And such a chase !

In each boat four sturdy men heaved upon as many ashen oars with mighty heaves, and our two dories shot ahead like live things. The caribou turned squarely up the lake and swam for dear life down the very center, in the face of wind and waves and pelting rain. He swam very fast, and it took us ten minutes to cut down, inch by inch, the hundred yards of water that separated us.

At last we overtook him, and ranged on either side of him as he swam, grunting and puffing; and then Fred, the guide, grabbed him by the horns. Instantly chaos arose and circled us. The lake lifted from its very bottom, shouldered over and fell about us with the hurtling rain, while the beating as of ten thousand hoofs rang upon the dory's side.

Above this tumult spoke a voice :

"Be careful and don't hurt him, Fred," it said.

That must have sounded ludicrous to Fred,

hanging on for dear life to that beast's antlers, while its sharp hoofs played a tattoo alternately upon his ribs and funny bone.

All the while I was standing in the bow of the other dory, taking pictures with reckless disregard of the swaying of the boat and the raindrops that sat stolidly upon my camera's one eye. In a moment of calm I obtained one fairly good photograph, but all those which should have shown the wonderful gymnastics that Fred and his captive indulged in came home from the Eastman Company blighted by that dismal word "failure."

After I had finished, Fred released the stag, and the way that poor brute legged it back across the lake was pitiful. We watched him till he took bottom and bounded out, and then we rowed onward.

The experience illustrated to us how easily the Newfoundlanders are enabled to catch the caribou as they swim across the waterways and cut their throats, as is their common custom.

A little later in the day, while searching for a passable channel up the shallow stream that connects the Middle and Upper Birchie Ponds, we were highly amused by the interest an old cow caribou evinced in our outfit. When first discovered by Keller she was feeding near by upon the bank. We landed within five hundred yards of her, and I shot a brace of yellow-leg plover, but she only looked more interested, and walked a few steps closer. We shouted, and waved our hats, but still she refused to run.

Late on the evening of the third day we found the spot we sought, an old Indian teepee that stood upon a point reaching half across the Upper Birchie Pond, about in its center.

"Where two sandy points stand opposite, there you must camp, for there the deer cross," we had been told by Mr. Parsons away back at our Grand Pond camp, and now we had found those points.

Without taking valuable time to reconnoiter, for the daylight was waning, we ascertained that the teepee was there, and thoroughly uninhabitable by white men or self-respecting dogs, and began hastily to make a temporary camp nearby. It had fortunately stopped raining, but everything was wet, ourselves included, and I for one hastened, as soon as camp was made, to dig up dry clothing from the bottom of one of the waterproof pack sacks; for, of course, what I wanted was at the bottom, where things one wants always are.

That evening we passed in pleasurable anticipation, and the glad knowledge that our ten days of traveling was at an end, and our destination reached. Tilley cooked our supper in the teepee, and served us the part the cockroaches didn't steal, and after several warmly contested games of California Jack, we turned in and slept to the musical patter of rain upon the canvas roof above us.

The sun was shooting flashing arrows of light through the pine tops when we awoke the next morning, and Tilley had our breakfast of caribou steak, golden plover and bacon waiting for us at the tent entrance.

It had been our intention to make permanent camp where we were, but fifteen minutes sufficed to convince us of the utter impossibility of such a course. This old Indian camping ground was a veritable slaughter pen. Beside the teepee were huge piles of bones, hide and skulls, some but half decomposed; and everywhere, in the woods and along the rocky shore, lay skulls and antlers. It is a low estimate to say that the horns of a thousand caribou lay bleaching beside that lake.

And there were some magnificent specimens, too ; but few that were not defaced and rendered valueless by the wanton ax of the Indian. The smaller heads were whole, but all the finer specimens were hacked and broken. In nine antlers out of ten could be seen the slugs of the Indians' sealing guns half buried in the bone.

It was evident that we dare not camp near that slaughter house, and so we hunted out a new site. We soon found one some distance away and directly upon the point, thirty yards back from the water and amongst the trees, that proved, after three hours' hard chopping and clearing, to be all it promised.

We stationed one of the men in an airy perch, forty feet up a pine, armed with a pair of field glasses and a whistle, and from that hour till we broke camp, as long as there was daylight, some one of the men was sure to be seated there, scanning the lake up and down for crossing bands of caribou.

When one was spied he blew the whistle. That was always the signal for a rush to the point, and we examined the bulls of the band from there through our glasses, and passed judgment upon them. If we decided they were desirable, the one whose turn it was seated himself in the canoe, his hunter took the paddle, and a spirited race began to see whether the bull or the boat would reach the prospective landing place first. Often it was the caribou, and when that proved the case the only recourse for the hunter was to hurriedly scramble ashore and take the chances of a long running shot.

It was the exception when caribou, once started across the lake, turned back again. Even if a human being was in view on the shore they were making for they would not return on their course, but would turn up or down the shore, and seek a second landing. If frustrated a second time, then they might swim back again, but seldom, indeed, did one turn at the first sign of danger.

It would be no difficult task to fill a book with our trip amidst the lakes and woodlands of Newfoundland. Indeed, I find the hardest thing to do is to condense my narrative into the small number of pages I am allowed. But, of course, I must not neglect the telling of my father's first kill. Like mine, it was witnessed by the entire party, and a very pretty bit of work it was.

We were just putting the finishing touches to our permanent camp, and Mr. Keller, father and myself, were debating as to the best method of constructing that very important article of camp furniture, the dining table, when the shrill alarum of the watch-tower whistle quivered and swelled in our ears.

Observing the courtesy of turn about, I handed my father his rifle and a half-dozen cartridges, and together we rushed to the point.

"There he blows!" called Elias from his watch-tower; and, following his leveled glasses, we descried the head and antlers of a bull moving rapidly toward our bank, a half-mile down the lake. Father and Tom Beaton sprang toward the canoe, and in a moment the dip, dip, of twin paddles met our waiting ears, and we saw the "Peterborough" stealing, like a thief in the night, down the shore, well within the shadow of the forest. I turned my attention to the bull. The glasses brought him almost to my feet. He was, indeed, a fine fellow, and swam so bravely, with eyes and nose water level, and antlers thrown regally

back, that I felt a momentary pity well up in
my breast.

The bull swam strongly on, unconscious of
danger; yet, more swiftly than he swam, his
doom flew down the shore. I could see my
father and Tom Beaton swaying rhythmically
to their work, putting their hearts into each
and every stroke. The canoe seemed alive.
Soon they had come within range, still unperceived. The caribou was making for a strip
of sand beach a few yards the other side of a
point that stretched far out in the lake.

The canoe rounded this point before the
deer saw it, and then, to our great surprise,
instead of landing there, where they would
have been offered a splendid shot as the bull
came ashore, they kept on, and, running between the deer and the bank, turned him
back.

Then began a race across the lake that was
as exciting as anything of the kind I have ever
seen. The caribou had a fifty-yard lead and
swam hard. At any part of the race, had my
father wished, he could have shot him easily,
but, of course, he did not. We upon the shore
guessed what he was doing. He was counting the points on the antlers, and deciding

whether that stag was killable! Rather novel, wasn't it? Examine your game, pass judgment, and then either kill or free it.

Two-thirds the distance was already consumed, then suddenly the canoe shot ahead and passed the caribou, then stopped, turned, and forced the poor beast back toward our side again.

They had decided the head was a desirable one, and now were driving the stag to the most convenient spot to kill him. They might easily have driven him to the very point we stood upon, but they were probably tired with their long and hard race, and simply returned him to the original point.

The stag swam slower now, and when within a hundred yards of the point the canoe again forged ahead, and this time my father stepped ashore upon the point. In a few seconds the caribou landed a hundred yards below him. For a fleeting moment he paused to shake himself. Brief as that moment was, it was fatal; for we, watching, saw a puff of creamy smoke suddenly appear before the leveled rifle, saw the bull plunge wildly a few yards and pitch headlong upon the beach, and before even the report of the shot reached us, we realized that the noble beast was dead.

I must pass over many interesting events in our camp life, and let it suffice to say that we lived every moment of it pleasantly.

Caribou were very plentiful, and it was not many days before our camp had assumed the semblance of a true hunter's paradise. On either side of our pathway before the tent stretched long lines of drying venison that the guides had laid claim to for their winter meat. This was a gratifying claim to us, for we were averse to wasting any part of the trophies of the chase, and the wants of a people who wintered in that bitter region were so great we knew we could not exceed them.

Beneath this drying meat hung the hides, all of which we preserved for rugs, and beneath and in front of these were the sawed and cleansed skulls and their glorious antlers. It was, indeed, a picture to gratify the exacting heart of a big game hunter; not because of the number of the kills, for that was not great, but because of their superior quality.

We had heard of the barrens above the hills about the lakes, but because of the heavy forest growth upon the hillsides, we could not see them from the lake shore. It was upon

these barrens that the monster stags were reported to roam, and we determined to visit
them before we broke camp.

Choosing a good day we made an early
start and were off. After an hour's row up
the lake, we landed at a spot where a clear
mountain brook babbled a promise of some
little aid to the ascent, and began what proved
to be the hardest bit of climbing I have ever
undergone. We used the ax freely, but in
spite of our efforts at opening a way, we consumed the better part of three hours in ascending less than a mile of sloping hillside.
It was crawl here and wriggle there, but never
an upright position among them all.

When at length we had reached the crest of
the hills, and no sign of the barrens appeared,
we sent a guide up a tree to reconnoiter. He
was able to make out very little, but said he
thought he saw an opening a mile inland.
This was discouraging; but while we were
discussing the advisability of beating a retreat,
one of the other guides, who had wandered
apart unperceived, returned with the gratifying news that not five hundred yards away lay
a huge plain literally alive with caribou. Instantly we resumed the march, rifles ready.

Now the trees began to thin, and the moss to grow more and more spongy, and then, with a suddenness which dazzled, the whole scene shifted, and we were standing in a fringe of breast-high bushes, and before us, as far as the eye could see, stretched a yellow waste of level plain, sweeping with gentle undulation to the north and east, where lay Grandfather's Lookout and Hall's Bay.

But our attention was chained by something nearer and more absorbing; for three hundred yards before us was a band of twenty caribou. There were three bulls. One, standing, was a little fellow. But two, lying down, were apparently monsters, one of them especially, and these two we decided to have. The cover extended fifty yards nearer to our quarry, and carefully we made our way to its very edge. The cows were browsing, and did not heed us. I do not believe they would have minded had we stepped fairly out into the open.

The biggest bull was to go to my father, as to date I held the champion head; and we agreed that he should fire first. He selected a stunted pine tree for a rest, and I stepped to one side, and chose the limb of another.

A Newfoundland Caribou Hunt

As he fired, I was conscious of seeing his bull stagger to its feet, and stand there swaying, and then my attention was absorbed by my own, which rose and started to trot away, side on. I fired, and apparently hit him, for he stopped instantly, and stood, head down, as if about to fall. I fired twice more, but the limb I used as a rest swayed and bothered me so that I missed each shot. Then I fired one shot off-hand, and the bull pitched forward all in a heap, with a bullet through his heart, quite dead.

My quarry disposed of, I turned to my father's. His bull still stood, apparently badly hurt and about to fall, but as the cows ran he started to follow, regaining new life at each step, until my father fired again, and the bull went down like a log.

We turned to the barrens, and a wonderful sight met our eyes. The whole plains were covered with grazing caribou. A half mile away one band roamed. A little farther three bulls, one of them a huge fellow, were daring one another to fight. Beyond stretched a waste with caribou everywhere.

There, before us, lay the two bulls we had just shot, with the cows that were with them

standing wondering by, having stopped running when the big bull fell. One cow lay just
beyond him, and we made sure the bullet that
felled this bull had also slain her. But, extraordinary to tell, we discovered she had quietly
lain down, and was not harmed at all. To
her the firing was a pleasant lullaby.

Father wished to try for the distant big
bull, and he and the guide, Tom, set out, leaving us to watch and wait. The wind was bad
for a successful stalk, and they were forced to
make a large circuit below the brow of the
plateau the barren rested upon. Soon they
were lost to sight.

Before they had been gone fifteen minutes,
the bull father had left for dead struggled to
his feet and started to walk away. I brought
him down again with a shot through the shoulder; but yet he was not dead, and when, later,
we walked up to him he attempted to charge
us, with many snorts of fury, and I was
obliged to send a bullet through his heart.

While father chased the bull I took several
photographs of the cows standing near by,
and then Keller and I walked a half mile to
the west, to where a spur of woods hid that
part of the plains from us.

A Newfoundland Caribou Hunt

We intended to head off my father's bull should he come that way, which was highly probable. But we saw nothing more of either the hunters or the bull till four o'clock in the afternoon, when the former returned and reported a kill after an extremely hard stalk of five miles, an exciting miss, and a splendid snap shot through the trees, when he had given up all hope of ever seeing that particular bull again.

From our new position we could see far to the west and north, and everywhere our glasses disclosed bands of feeding caribou. The plain was literally honeycombed with countless game trails that resembled wagon roads more than paths. And everywhere the level reach was dotted with silver ponds and lakes. It was a wonderful sight, the most marvelous I have ever seen, and we spent an hour viewing it.

Then we returned to the slain bulls, and, after literally driving the cows away, for one of them lay quite still until we were within thirty yards of her, we began skinning out.

We arrived in camp late that night, tired with the exhausting tramp down hill in the dark through the thickest of woods, but pleased beyond measure by our day's experience and trophies. On the morrow we sent three of the men to chop a trail up to the barrens, and ever after that, when we paid the plains a visit, we had a good road to ascend by.

One Sunday my father went on an exploring expedition to the head of the lake, and returned at night with a strange tale. He had followed a creek, as he said, "way up into Hall's Bay country," and had determined to his satisfaction that, contrary to his belief, the deer did not use that end of the lake as a pass to cross southward. But he made a discovery that explained a good many things mystifying to us. Where the creek he followed entered the lake were erected three huge scaffolds, one of which was as large as the floor of a big house. These structures were of considerable age, but in good repair, and were the drying scaffolds of the Mic-Mac Indians. Here they prepared their annual stock of winter meat, killing it around the shores of the lake, and floating it down. It was a certainty from the signs in evidence about these scaffolds that thousands of caribou were annually dried there. That this lake

had also been a hunting ground for white men
for years and years was proven to us by my
finding, neatly carven in the huge trunk of a
fallen forest monarch, the date 1847, and three
initials that I have now forgotten.

We enjoyed a number of amusing incidents
where caribou literally came into camp, and
once, in particular, Erie, the big Newfoundland puppy, and Tilley, the cook, came face to
face with a yearling, and almost took it alive;
but it finally got into the water and escaped.

I wish to recount two more kills—our last.
Both were made upon the barren; and we
prize their heads highly. I shall relate father's kill in his own words, as he told the
story, late in the evening, after his triumphant
return.

" It was almost dark," he said, " and Tom
and Elias had gone back to get those other
heads. I waited alone at the edge of a point
of pines. Presently a cow and a big bull
walked leisurely into view four hundred yards
below me. I determined to have those antlers, for even in the fading light I could see
that they were grand ones; but the distance
was too great to risk a shot. I began a cautious stalk; but I had not gone a dozen steps

when the cow saw me and bolted, with the bull after her.

"As they disappeared I yelled at them, never expecting to see either of them again. Imagine my surprise when the old bull stepped forth from the woods above and grunted at me. I shouted again and waved my hat, and the fellow grunted more fiercely still, and started for me. I stepped forward to meet him half-way, when back he skipped into the woods. In a moment he was out again, and for five minutes he and I kept up that dance. I decided that before long he would bolt, as he had evidently given up his idea of charging me, and so I determined to risk a shot.

"The distance was great, pacing 365 yards, and the light almost gone. In addition to that the caribou stood face on and hidden from the shoulder down by a bush. I thought he stood in the very edge of the woods. Raising my .303, I held squarely for his forehead between the eyes and fired. He disappeared instantly.

"'He's gone now,' I told myself. But I had expected to miss, and did not feel very badly, considering the circumstances. But I walked to where he stood, and to my surprise and delight, there he lay in his tracks, stone dead. My bullet had passed directly through the left brow plow, cutting a clean hole three inches long, and smashed into his brain, killing him instantly."

My last kill was made the following day, the last in camp. It was pouring rain and very foggy, but I set forth with Tom, Fred and Elias, and arrived upon the barrens about noon. What a bleak prospect it was! The steady rains of the past week had flooded the entire plain with icy water, above which the wiry grasses waved mournfully. The fine rain drove almost level before a fierce north wind, and a thin gray fog obscured clear vision. But we determined not to give up, and, leaving Fred and Elias to skin out the kill of the night previous, Tom and I set forth, splashing across the plain. We had gone perhaps a half mile, and had just breasted the brow of a swell, when simultaneously we both ducked low, and hurriedly ran down the hill again.

We had discovered a band of thirty or more caribou feeding a mile beyond us. Our glasses showed three bulls, two of them very large, and we held a war consultation.

To begin with, the wind was wrong. Then

there was absolutely no cover, and the plain between the caribou and ourselves was dead level. To make a circle sufficient to obtain cover meant a three-mile tramp, with the prospect that the caribou would be gone when we got to the end of it. So we decided to go a short distance to the right to avoid having the wind blow directly from us to the animals, and then to crawl up on them over the flat and open barren.

I now did a very foolish thing. It was bitterly cold, and the water was icy, but I threw aside my gloves, nor'wester hat, and mackintosh topcoat, and began my stalk with naked head, and hands and body covered by only a thin flannel shirt. For a solid hour we wriggled forward inch by inch, through the rain and fog, stopping every time a cow raised her head. Flat on our stomachs we squirmed along, and in that position, more in the mud and water than out, we covered the best part of a mile.

Long before we had crawled near enough to be in anything like passable range a fourth bull joined the herd, and immediately a fight began. The biggest of the three original bulls attacked him, and they closed, and for fifteen minutes we lay still and watched them trample the ground as they struggled this way and that for the mastery. The clashing of their horns was like the ringing of sabres, and I cannot understand why they did not break them to atoms.

If it had not been for the cows standing interestedly about, we could no doubt have run directly up to the fighting bulls unperceived. At last the interloper was whipped off, and, walking a little to one side, he lay down and was lost to sight. But we had seen enough of him to determine that he was the one we wanted, and again we began our crawl. My hands were numb and swollen with the cold and the rough usage I had given them, but I passed my rifle forward to Tom to lug, and kept on.

Soon we were within range, but it was impossible, because of the fog, to say whether the distance was two or four hundred yards. The herd had fed into a clump of low bushes that promised us some sort of cover, and now we advanced more rapidly. We crawled through their very center, once dropping flat in four inches of water, while an old cow walked leisurely about us not twenty feet

away. Then she fed away again, and we
wriggled on.

We knew now that we were very near the
bull we sought, but still we could not see him.
Suddenly a cow took fright and trotted away.
Several more followed her, and then, eighty
yards in front of us, our bull arose. He
stood face on, all but his head hidden by the
bush.

Three separate times I tried to catch a sure
sight, but I was shaking so violently with the
cold, and my hands were so numb that the
rifle traveled all over the face of the landscape, but never rested for a fleeting moment
on the caribou.

Then I deliberately laid my Winchester
down, rolled over on my side, and pushed my
frozen hands into the breast of Tom's warm
shirt. For fully two minutes I kept them
there. The band had run a hundred yards
and stopped, and our bull still stood watching
us. Then he suddenly wheeled, and ran pellmell for the woods four hundred yards away,
and we saw the band break and run in the
opposite direction. Fred and Elias had finished their job and were coming to seek us,
and they had frightened our quarry.

A Newfoundland Caribou Hunt

I withdrew my partially warmed fingers in a hurry, seized my rifle, sprang to my feet, and opened fire. The caribou was running two-thirds quartering from me, and it was very difficult shooting in the driving rain and fog. I emptied my magazine of its five shots, thrust in two more, and fired them, and just as I discharged the last cartridge the bull disappeared in the fringe of the woods.

I turned about to try a shot at the others, but they were gone.

We walked to the spot where we had last seen our deer, and, pleasant to relate, there he lay, dead, with five shots through the body and two through the antlers. These were magnificent in symmetry and coloring, and of very good dimensions; and were the handsomest set I ever saw. The brow plows were uniform in size, with fingers interlaced; and on either side above them, from a wide, flat surface, sprang two veritable hands, each having five long spreading fingers. The main beams curved far forward and over, and their numerous points recalled some strange barbaric musical instrument. The entire horns were tinted a rich, reddish amber, like the coloring of meerschaum.

My first shot was fired at 105 yards, and my last at 390.

We skinned the prize and faced campward in triumph. Twice we sighted bands of caribou, but we left them in peace. We had enough.

The next day we broke camp, and began our homeward journey; and the trophies of our hunt now adorn the St. Louis Club.

Clay Arthur Pierce.

BIRD'S-EYE VIEW OF THE PROPOSED ZOOLOGICAL PARK.

From a Photograph of the Society's Topographic Model.

The Origin of the New York Zoölogical Society

In the autumn of 1894 I entered into a correspondence with Mr. Theodore Roosevelt, the President of the Boone and Crockett Club, with reference to securing, during the coming session of the Assembly, certain legislation in the interest of game protection. It was finally decided that the subject should be laid before the Club for its sanction; and this was done at the annual meeting of the Boone and Crockett Club of January 16, 1895, when the matter was entrusted to a committee of which I was chairman.

One of the chief objects of this committee was to secure for New York City, which was then entering into a new era of expansion under a reform administration, a zoölogical park on lines entirely divergent from the Old World zoölogical gardens, and which would tend to introduce those principles of game preservation advocated by the Boone and Crockett Club.

313

Trail and Camp-Fire

Upon investigation, the committee found
that a measure had already been introduced
at Albany, providing for the establishment of
a zoölogical park on city lands, located north
of 155th Street. This bill had been introduced for several years in succession by Mr.
Andrew H. Green, and had each year been
defeated, chiefly on account of a clause in it
which authorized the New York Park Board
to turn over the existing Central Park Men-
agerie to the proposed Society. This clause
had provoked violent opposition from certain
East Side representatives, who declared the
bill to be a mere attempt to secure the control
and removal of the Central Park Zoo, and so
to deprive the poor children of the pleasure
afforded by it. The strength of this opposition was good evidence of the popularity of
any sort of animal collection, for a more
wretched exhibition of ill-kept specimens than
the existing Zoo cannot be found in any large
city in the world.

Curiously enough, there was also in circula-
tion a rumor that the proposed Society would
engage in the business of breeding small animals, such as dogs and fowls, to the lasting
injury of the small animal dealers.

The New York Zoölogical Society

Mr. Green was interviewed by the committee, and, realizing that the bill could not succeed without the help of the Boone and Crockett Club, he agreed to give them the control of the new Society if the bill should become law.

The measure was in charge of Assemblyman W. W. Niles, Jr., who represented the district above the Harlem River, in which the proposed park would in all probability be located. He consented to push the bill, if the Boone and Crockett Club would assume the responsibility of organizing the Society, and if some of the members would appear as incorporators.

The bill was therefore amended by the insertion of the names of two Boone and Crockett Club men, Mr. La Farge and myself, among the original incorporators, and Mr. Niles modified the clause relating to the Central Park Zoo in such a manner that while the opposition was appeased, the Society nevertheless retained the right to a preference in case the Park Board disposed of the existing Zoo at any time in the future. The small animal dealers were interviewed by the committee, and their fears dispelled. Mr. Niles then pushed the bill with vigor, and, after a prolonged contest, he succeeded in forcing it through by dint of some of the hardest work done at Albany that year.

The Society was organized May 7, 1895, and the first board of managers contained the names of nine Boone and Crockett Club members, including the vice-president and both the secretaries.

Nearly a year was spent in the consideration of various sites, and the southern end of Bronx Park was finally found to possess almost the exact landscape features deemed essential by the experts to whom the available locations were referred. In Bronx Park, meadow, glade, forest, pond and river were so distributed that buildings could be located and collections installed, practically without injury to existing trees.

After a searching inquiry into the question of accessibility, drainage and kindred matters, the Zoölogical Society approved this site, and on May 21, 1896, formal application was made to the Commissioners of the Sinking Fund under the terms of the Society's charter.

The question was under consideration by the city authorities for nearly ten months,

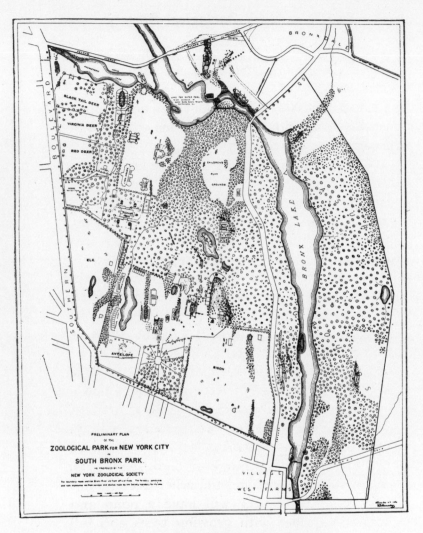

PRELIMINARY PLAN OF THE NEW YORK ZOO.

Showing Disposition of American Mammals.

The New York Zoölogical Society

and in March, 1897, a grant was made by the city to the New York Zoölogical Society of all that portion of Bronx Park lying south of Pelham Avenue, being about 261 acres, upon certain restrictions and conditions entirely satisfactory to the Society.

A bill was also secured from the Legislature at Albany providing $125,000 for the preparation of the land to receive the Society's buildings and collections. At the present writing the Society numbers 425 members, and is in a most prosperous financial condition.

As the New York Zoölogical Society owes its existence to the Boone and Crockett Club, a few words concerning its purposes cannot be amiss. Its primary object is to secure herds— not merely individuals—of each of the large North American quadrupeds, and to place them as far as possible in surroundings identical with or closely resembling their natural habitats. A space of twenty acres will be devoted to the American bison; the moose will have a wooded range of eight acres; the wapiti fifteen acres, and the other deer similar ranges. The beaver will have a pond and stream, together with growing trees and full opportunity to build his dam and cabins, while the bears will be quartered in rock ledges and caves. A flying aviary, 150 feet long, 75 feet wide and 50 feet high, will enable the flamingos, herons, ibis, and egrets to retain their strength by the free use of their wings; and the monkeys will have an entire grove of trees at their disposal—fenced in by a high wire netting, to be sure, but still giving them freedom on a scale never before attempted.

The first work of the Society will be to present the larger North American mammals in such a way that they can be studied by the public, and still keep themselves in perfect condition by exercise. After that the larger buildings will be constructed, one after another, until a zoölogical park shall be developed on strictly American lines. By this is meant the absolute preservation of all desirable natural features now existing, and the subordination of all structures and of landscape treatment to the needs of the specimens, and especially to the ranges of the larger animals.

The largest Zoo in existence in Europe is the Zoölogical Garden in Berlin—sixty acres in extent, while the National Zoölogical Park at Washington contains 168 acres, much of which, however, is unsuitable for collections,

so with its 261 acres and room to grow,
the New York Zoölogical Society begins its
career with an enormous advantage.

Admission to the Park will be free—except
on two days of each week, when a small admission fee will be charged—but in return,
the city will be expected to supply the cost
of maintenance. The Society will supply the
collections and scientific management of the
Park, and, so far as practicable, the buildings.

The advantages of membership in the Society include not only free admission and
tickets for guests, but certain right to publications, use of library, and other advantages.

Scientific investigations, publications, lec-
tures and animal art exhibitions will be carried
on by the Society in conjunction with the
Park, and there is every reason to hope that,
in the near future, New York will have a
flourishing rival to the London Zoölogical
Society.

The committee of this club, which had in
charge the introduction of this enterprise, at-
tribute their success before the Legislature to
the energetic help of members of the Boone
and Crockett Club, and to the very considerable influence of the club itself. When the

Society was once organized, the first support it secured was from the members of that club, who came forward almost in a body—practically every New York City member—with money and with time.

The formation of this Society comes at a time when it is still possible to secure specimens for a great collection. It may be confidently asserted that twenty-five years hence the rinderpest and repeating rifle will have destroyed most, if not all, of the larger African fauna—including certainly the most beautiful antelopes in the world—and game in India and North America in a wild state will almost have ceased to exist.

The New York Zoölogical Society, the most vigorous offspring of this club, demonstrates what a mission and opportunity the Boone and Crockett Club has in these closing days of the century in its efforts to preserve the game and the forests; in short, to preserve to future generations some remnant of the heritage which was our fathers', and which, to a great extent, still is ours, though so few of us have learned to estimate it at its true value.

Madison Grant.

Books on Big Game

The nineteenth century has been, beyond all others, the century of big game hunters, and of books about big game. From the days of Nimrod to our own there have been mighty hunters before the Lord, and most warlike and masterful races have taken kindly to the chase, as chief among those rough pastimes which appeal naturally to men with plenty of red blood in their veins. But until the present century the difficulties of travel were so great that men with a taste for sport could rarely gratify this taste except in their own neighborhood. There was good hunting in Macedonia in the days of Alexander the Great; there was good hunting in the Hercynnian forest when Frank and Burgund were turning Gaul into France; there was good hunting in Lithuania as late as the days of the Polish Commonwealth; but the most famous kings and nobles of Europe, within historic times, though they might kill the aurochs and the bison, the bear and the boar, had no chance to test their prowess against the mightier and more terrible beasts of the tropics. No modern man could be more devoted to the chase than were the territorial lords of the Middle Ages, and their successors in continental Europe to the beginning of the present century; indeed, they erred generally on the side of fantastic extravagance and exaggeration in their favorite pursuit, turning it into a solemn and rather ridiculous business instead of a healthy and vigorous pastime; but they could hunt only the beasts of their own forests. The men who went on long voyages usually had quite enough to do simply as travelers; the occupation of getting into unknown lands was in itself sufficiently absorbing and hazardous to exclude any chance of combining with it the rôle of sportsman.

With the present century all this has changed. Even in the last century it began to change. The Dutch settlers at the Cape of Good Hope, and the English settlers on the Atlantic coast of North America, found themselves thrown back into a stage of life where hunting was one of the main means of livelihood, as well as the most exciting and adventurous of pastimes. These men knew the chase as no men of their race had known it since the days before history dawned; and until the closing decades of the present century, the American and the Afrikander of the frontier largely led the lives of professional hunters. Oom Paul and Buffalo Bill have had very different careers since they reached middle age; but in their youth warfare against wild beasts and wild men was the most serious part of the life work of both. They and their fellows did the rough pioneer work of civilization, under conditions which have now vanished for ever; and their type will perish with the passing of the forces that called it into being. But the big game hunter, whose campaigns against big game are not simply incidents in his career as a pioneer settler, will remain with us for some time longer; and it is of him and his writings that we wish to treat.

Toward the end of the last century this big game hunter had already appeared, although, like all early types, he was not yet thoroughly specialized. Le Vail-

Books on Big Game

lant hunted in South Africa, and his book is excellent reading now. A still better book is that of Bruce, the Abyssinian explorer, who was a kind of Burton of his days, with a marvelous faculty for getting into quarrels, but an even more marvelous faculty for doing work which no other man could do. He really opened a new world to European men of letters and science; who thereupon promptly united in disbelieving all he said, though they were credulous enough toward people who really should have been distrusted. But his tales have been proved true by many an explorer since then, and his book will always possess interest for big game hunters, because of his experiences in the chase. Sometimes he shot merely in self-defense or for food, but he also made regular hunting trips in company with the wild lords of the shifting frontier between dusky Christian and dusky infidel. He feasted in their cane palaces, where the walls were hung with the trophies of giant game, and in their company, with horse and spear, he attacked and overcame the buffalo and the rhinoceros.

By the beginning of the present century the hunting book proper became differentiated, as it were, from the book of the explorer. One of the earliest was Williamson's "Oriental Field Sports." This is to the present day a most satisfactory book, especially to sporting parents with large families of small children. The pictures are all in colors, and the foliage is so very green, and the tigers are so very red, and the boars so very black, and the tragedies so uncommonly vivid and startling, that for the youthful mind the book really has no formidable rival outside of the charmed circle where Slovenly Peter stands first.

Trail and Camp-Fire

Since then multitudes of books have been written about big game hunting. Most of them are bad, of course, just as most novels and most poems are bad ; but some of them are very good indeed, while a few are entitled to rank high in literature—though it cannot be said that as yet big game hunters as a whole have produced such writers as those who dwell on the homelier and less grandiose side of nature. They have not produced a White or Burroughs, for instance. What could not Burroughs have done if only he had cared for adventure and for the rifle, and had roamed across the Great Plains and the Rockies, and through the dim forests, as he has wandered along the banks of the Hudson and the Potomac ! Thoreau, it is true, did go to the Maine Woods ; but then Thoreau was a transcendentalist, and, therefore, slightly anæmic. A man must feel the beat of hardy life in his veins before he can be a good big game hunter. Fortunately, Richard Jefferies has written an altogether charming little volume on the Red Deer, so that there is, at least, one game animal which has been fully described by a man of letters, who was also both a naturalist and a sportsman ; but it is irritating to think that no one has done as much for the lordlier game of the wilderness. Not only should the hunter be able to describe vividly the chase, and the life habits of the quarry, but he should also draw the wilderness itself, and the life of those who dwell or sojourn therein. We wish to see before us the cautious stalk and the headlong gallop ; the great beasts as they feed or rest or run or fight ; the wild hunting camps ; the endless plains shimmering in the sunlight ; the vast solemn forests ; the desert and the marsh and the mountain chain ; and all

Books on Big Game

that lies hidden in the lonely lands through which the wilderness wanderer roams and hunts game.

But there remain a goodly number of books which are not merely filled with truthful information of importance, but which are also absorbingly interesting; and if a book is both truthful and interesting it is surely entitled to a place somewhere in general literature. Unfortunately, the first requisite bars out a great many hunting books. There are not a few mighty hunters, who have left long records of their achievements, and who undoubtedly did achieve a great deal; but who contrive to leave in the mind of the reader the uncomfortable suspicion, that beside their prowess with the rifle they were skilled in the use of that more archaic weapon the long bow. Gerard was a great lion killer; but some of his accounts of the lives, deaths, and especially the courtships, of lions, bear much less relation to actual facts than do the novels of Dumas. Not a few of the productions of hunters of this type should be grouped under the head-lines used by the newspapers of our native land in describing something which they are perfectly sure hasn't happened—"Important, if True."

If we were limited to the choice of one big game writer, we should have to choose Sir Samuel Baker, for his experiences are very wide, and we can accept without question all that he says in his books. He hunted in India, in Africa, and in North America; he killed all the chief kinds of heavy and dangerous game; and he followed them on foot and on horseback, with the rifle and the knife, and with hounds. For the same reason if we could choose but one work, it would have to be the volumes of "Big Game Shooting" in the Badminton Library, edited by Mr. Phillipps Wolley—himself a man who has written well of big game hunting in out of the way places, from the Caucasus to the Cascades. These volumes contain pieces by many different authors; but they differ from most volumes of the kind in that all the writers are trustworthy and interesting; though the palm must be given to Oswell's delightful account of his South African hunting.

In all these books the one point to be insisted on is that a big game hunter has nothing in common with so many of the men who delight to call themselves sportsmen. Sir Samuel Baker has left a very amusing record of the horror he felt for the Ceylon sportsmen who, by the term "sport," meant horse-racing instead of elephant shooting. Half a century ago, Gordon Cumming wrote of "the life of the wild hunter, so far preferable to that of the mere sportsman"; and his justification for this somewhat sneering reference to the man who takes his sport in too artificial a manner, may be found in the pages of a then noted authority on such sports as horse-racing and fox-hunting; for in Apperly's "Nimrod Abroad," in the course of an article on the game of the American wilderness, there occurs this delicious sentence : "A damper, however, is thrown over all systems of deerstalking in Canada by the necessity, which is said to be unavoidable, of bivouacking in the woods instead of in well-aired sheets!" Verily, there was a great gulf between the two men.

In the present century the world has known three great hunting-grounds : Africa, from the equator to the southernmost point; India, both farther and hither; and North America west of the Mississippi, from the Rio

Books on Big Game

Grande to the Arctic Circle. The atter never approached either of the former in the wealth and variety of the species, or in the size and terror of the chief beasts of the chase; but it surpassed India in the countless numbers of the individual animals, and in the wild and unknown nature of the hunting-grounds.

South Africa was the true hunter's paradise. If the happy hunting-grounds were to be found anywhere on this world, they lay between the Orange and the Zambesi, and extended northward here and there to the Nile countries and Somaliland. Nowhere else were there such multitudes of game, representing so many and such widely different kinds of animals, of such size, such beauty, such infinite variety. We should have to go back to the fauna of the Pleistocene to find its equal. Never before did men enjoy such hunting as fell to the lot of those roving adventurers, who first penetrated its hidden fastnesses, camped by its shrunken rivers, and galloped across its sun-scorched wastes; and, alas that it should be written, no man will ever see the like again. Fortunately, its memory will forever be kept alive in some of the books that the great hunters have written about it, such as Cornwallis Harris's "Wild Sports of South Africa," Gordon Cumming's "Hunter's Life in South Africa," Baldwin's "African Hunting," Drummond's "Large Game and Natural History of South Africa," and, best of all, Selous's two books, "A Hunter's Wanderings in South Africa," and "Travel and Adventure in Southeast Africa." Selous is the last of the great hunters, and no other has left books of such value as his.

Moreover, the pencil has done its part as well as the pen. Harris, who was the pioneer of all the hunters, published an admirable folio entitled "The Game and Wild Animals of South Africa." It is perhaps of more value than any other single work. J. G. Millais, in "A Breath from the Veldt," has rendered a unique service, not only by his charming descriptions, but by his really extraordinary sketches of the South African antelopes, both at rest, and in every imaginable form of motion. Nearly at the other end of the continent there is an admirable book on lion-hunting in Somaliland, by Captain C. J. Melliss. Much information about big game can be taken from the books of various missionaries and explorers; Livingstone and Du Chaillu doing for Africa in this respect what Catlin did for North America.

As we have said before, one great merit of these books is that they are interesting. Quite a number of men who are good sportsmen, as well as men of means, have written books about their experiences in Africa; but the trouble with too many of these short and simple annals of the rich is, that they are very dull. They are not literature, any more than treatises on farriery and cooking are literature. To read a mere itinerary is like reading a guide book. No great enthusiasm in the reader can be roused by such a statement as "this day walked twenty-three miles, shot one giraffe and two zebras; porter deserted with the load containing the spare boots"; and the most exciting events, if chronicled simply as "shot three rhinos and two buffalo; the first rhino and both buffalo charged," become about as thrilling as a paragraph in Baedeker. There is no need of additional literature of the guide-book and cookery-book kind. "Fine writing" is, of course, abhorrent in a way that is not possible for mere baldness of statement, and

Books on Big Game

would-be "funny" writing is even worse, as it almost
invariably denotes a certain underbred quality of mind;
but there is need of a certain amount of detail, and of
vivid and graphic, though simple, description. In other
words, the writer on big game should avoid equally Carlyle's theory and Carlyle's practice in the matter of
verbosity.

Really good game books are sure to contain descriptions which linger in the mind just like one's pet passages in any other good book. One example is Selous's
account of his night watch close to the wagon when, in
the pitchy darkness, he killed three of the five lions which
had attacked his oxen; or his extraordinary experience
while hunting elephants on a stallion who turned sulky,
and declined to gallop out of danger. The same is true
of Drummond's descriptions of the camps of native hunting parties, of tracking wounded buffalo through the
reeds, and of waiting for rhinos by a desert pool under
the brilliancy of the South African moon; descriptions,
by the way, which show that the power of writing inter-
estingly is not dependent upon even approximate cor-
rectness in style, for some of Mr. Drummond's sentences,
in point of length and involution, would compare not unfavorably with those of a Populist Senator discussing
bimetalism.

The experiences of a hunter in Africa, with its teeming
wealth of strange and uncouth beasts, must have been,
and in places must still be, about what one's experience
would be if one could suddenly go back a few hundred
thousand years for a hunting trip in the Pliocene or
Pleistocene. In Mr. Astor Chanler's book, " Through
Jungle and Desert," the record of his trip through the

329

melancholy reed beds of the Guaso Nyiro, and of his
return journey, carrying his wounded companion, through
regions where the caravan was perpetually charged by
rhinoceros, reads like a bit out of the unreckoned ages
of the past, before the huge and fierce monsters of old
had vanished from the earth, or acknowledged man as
their master. Another excellent book of mixed hunting
and scientific exploration is Mr. Donaldson Smith's
"Through Unknown African Countries." If anything,
the hunting part is unduly sacrificed to some of the
minor scientific work. Full knowledge of a new breed
of rhinoceros, or a full description of the life history and
chase of almost any kind of big game, is worth more than
any quantity of new spiders and scorpions. Birds and
insects remain in the land, and can always be described
by the shoal of scientific investigators who follow the
first adventurous explorers; but it is only the pioneer
hunter who can tell us all about the far more interesting
and important beasts of the chase, the different kinds of
big game, and especially dangerous big game; and it is a
mistake in any way to subordinate the greater work to
the lesser.

Books on big game hunting in India are as plentiful,
and as good, as those about Africa. Forsyth's " Highlands of Central India," Sanderson's " Thirteen Years
Among the Wild Beasts of India," Shakespeare's " Wild
Sports of India," and Kinloch's " Large Game Shooting,"
are perhaps the best; but there are many other writers,
like Baldwin, Rice, Macintyre, and Stone, who are also
very good. Indeed, to try to give even the titles of the
good books on Indian shooting would make a magazine
article read too much like the Homeric catalogue of

Books on Big Game

ships, or the biblical generations of the Jewish patriarchs.
The four books singled out for special reference are interesting reading for any one; particularly the accounts
of the deaths of man-eating tigers at the hands of Forsyth, Shakespeare, and Sanderson, and some of Kinloch's Himalayan stalks. It is indeed royal sport which
the hunter has among the stupendous mountain masses
of the Himalayas, or in the rank jungles and steamy
tropical forests of India.

Hunting should go hand in hand with the love of
natural history, as well as with descriptive and narrative
power. Hornaday's "Two Years in the Jungle" is
especially interesting to the naturalist; but he adds not a
little to our knowledge of big game. It is earnestly to
be wished that some hunter will do for the gorilla what
Hornaday has done for the great East Indian ape, the
mias or orang.

There are many good books on American big game,
but, rather curiously, they are for the most part modern.
Until within the present generation Americans only
hunted big game if they were frontier settlers, professional trappers, southern planters, army officers, or explorers. The people of the cities of the old States were
bred in the pleasing faith that anything unconnected
with business was both a waste of time and presumably
immoral. Those who traveled went to Europe instead
of to the Rocky Mountains.

There are good descriptions of big game hunting in
the books of writers like Catlin, but they come in incidentally. Elliott's book on "Carolina Field Sports" is
admirable, although the best chapters are on harpooning
the devil-fish; and John Palliser, an Englishman, in his

"Solitary Hunter," has given us the best description of hunting in the far West, when it was still an untrodden wilderness. Unfortunately, the old hunters themselves, the men who had most experience in the life of the wilderness, were utterly unable to write about it; they could not tell what they had seen or done. Occasional attempts have been made to get noted hunters to write books, either personally or by proxy, but these attempts have not been successful.

The first effort to get men of means and cultivation in the northern and eastern States of the Union to look at field sports in the right light was made by an Englishman who wrote over the signature of Frank Forrester. He did a great deal for the shotgun men; but, unfortunately, he was a true cockney, who cared little for really wild sports, and he was afflicted with that dreadful pedantry which pays more heed to ceremonial and terminology than to the thing itself. He was sincerely distressed because the male of the ordinary American deer was called a buck instead of a stag; and it seemed to him to be a matter of moment whether one spoke of a "gang" or a "herd" of elk.

There are plenty of excellent books nowadays, however—Dodge's "Hunting Grounds of the Great West," Caton's "Deer and Antelope of America," Van Dyke's "Still Hunter," and the *Century's* "Sport with Gun and Rod," for instance. Warburton Pike, Caspar Whitney, and Frederick Schwatka have given a pretty full account of boreal sports; and Pendarves Vivian and Baillie Grohman have written exceedingly interesting accounts of hunting trips in the Rockies. A new departure, that of photographing wild animals in their homes, was taken in

Books on Big Game

Wallihan's "Hoofs, Claws and Antlers," although Mr. Wallihan greatly marred the book by combining with the genuine photographs of wild game a number of "faked" pictures of stuffed animals. Finally, in Parkman's "Oregon Trail" and Irving's "Trip on the Prairie," two great writers have left us a lasting record of the free life of the rifle-bearing wanderers who first hunted in the wild western lands.

Of course, there are plenty of books on European game. Scrope's "Art of Deerstalking," Bromley Davenport's "Sport," and all the books of Charles St. John, are classic. The chase of the wolf and boar is excellently described by an unnamed writer in "Wolf Hunting and Wild Sports of Brittany." Baillie Grohman's "Sport in the Alps" is devoted to the mountain game of Central Europe, and is, moreover, a mine of curious hunting lore, most of which is entirely new to men unacquainted with the history of the chase in Continental Europe during the last few centuries. An entirely novel type of adventure is set forth in Lamont's "Seasons with the Sea Horses," wherein he describes his hunting in arctic waters with rifle and harpoon. Lloyd's "Scandinavian Adventures" and "Northern Field Sports," and Whishaw's "Out of Doors in Tsar Land," tell of the life and game of the snowy northern forests. Chapman has done good work for both Norway and Spain.

Finally, we come to a book which, quite unconsciously, gives us the exact model of what a big game hunter and a true sportsman, who is much more than a mere sportsman, should be. I mean Mr. Edward North Buxton's "Short Stalks." It is the book of a man who is a hardy lover of nature, a skilled hunter, but not a game butcher;

333

a man who has too much serious work on hand ever to let himself become a mere globe-trotting rifleman. We are not disposed to undervalue manly outdoor sports, or to fail to appreciate the advantage to a nation, as well as to an individual, of such pastimes; but they must be pastimes, and not business, and they must not be carried to excess. There is a good deal to be said for the life of a professional hunter in lonely lands; but the man able to be something more, should be that something more— an explorer, a naturalist, or else a man who makes his hunting trips merely delightful interludes in his life work. As for excessive game butchery, it amounts merely to a debauch. The man whose chief title to glory is that, during an industrious career of destruction, he has slaughtered 200,000 head of deer and partridges, stands unpleasantly near those continental kings and nobles who, during the centuries before the French Revolution, deified the chase of the stag, and made it into a highly artificial cult, which they followed to the exclusion of state-craft and war-craft and everything else. James, the founder of the ignoble English branch of the Stuart kings, as unkingly a man as ever sat on a throne, was fanatical in his devotion to the artificial kind of chase which then absorbed the souls of the magnates of continental Europe.

There is no need to exercise much patience with men who protest against field sports; unless, indeed, they are logical vegetarians of the flabbiest Hindoo type. If it is morally right to kill an animal to eat its body, then it is morally right to kill it to preserve its head. A good sportsman will not hesitate as to the relative value he puts upon the two, and to get the one he will go a long time without eating the other. No nation facing the unhealthy softening and relaxation of fibre which tend to accompany civilization can afford to neglect anything that will develop hardihood, resolution, and the scorn of discomfort and danger. But if sport is made an end instead of a means, it is better to avoid it altogether. The greatest stag-hunter of the seventeenth century was the Elector of Saxony. During the Thirty Years' War he killed some 80,000 deer and boar. Now, if there ever was a time when the ruler of a country needed to apply himself to serious matters, it was during the Thirty Years' War in Germany, and if the Elector in question had eschewed hunting he might have compared more favorably with Gustavus Adolphus, Tilly and Wallenstein.

Wellington was fond of fox-hunting, but he did very little of it during the period of the Peninsular War. Grant cared much for fine horses, but he devoted his attention to other matters when facing Lee before Richmond. Perhaps as good an illustration as could be wished of the effects of the opposite course is furnished by poor Louis XVI. He took his sport more seriously than he did his position as ruler of his people. On the day when the revolutionary mob came to Versailles, he merely recorded in his diary that he had "gone out shooting, and had killed eighty-one head when he was interrupted by events." The particular event to which this "interruption" led up was the guillotine. Not many sportsmen have to face such a possibility; but they do run the risk of becoming a curse to themselves and to every one else, if they once get into the frame of mind which can look on the business of life as merely an interruption to sport.

LIST OF BOOKS

Written by members of the Boone and Crockett Club on Hunting, Exploration, Natural History, etc.

CAPT. HENRY T. ALLEN. *Reconnaissance in Alaska.*

An account of an exploring expedition through hitherto unknown portions of Alaska, with notes on the Indians, game and natural history.

EDWARD NORTH BUXTON. *Short Stalks.*

An account of sport with the rifle, carried on in the most sportsmanlike way, not only in the Rocky Mountaines, the Pyrenees and Scandinavia, but in such out-of-the-way places as the Atlas Mountains, Asia Minor and Sardinia.

JUDGE JOHN DEAN CATON, LL.D. *Antelope and Deer of America.*

A very full description of the physical characteristics, life, habits and chase of the prong-buck, and of all the North American deer; the accounts of the wapiti, mule deer and white-tail deer, both in their wild state and in captivity, being particularly good.

336

List of Books

WILLIAM ASTOR CHANLER. *Through Jungle and Desert.*

An account of an adventurous exploring expedition into an unknown region of East Africa, with many notes on the geography and ethnology of the country traversed. Incidentally there is much about hunting the teeming herds of great game, such as rhinoceros, giraffe, zebra, and the various antelopes. One of the antelope secured proved to be a new species.

GEN. RICHARD IRVING DODGE. *Hunting Grounds of the Great West.*

A full account of life and the chase on the great plains in the old days, when they were still the jealously guarded hunting grounds of the Horse Indians, and were still roamed over by myriads of bison.

Our Wild Indians.

A full description of the Horse Indians of the great plains, in peace and war, as seen by one of the soldiers who fought against or beside them for many years.

GEN. A. W. GREELY. *Three Years of Arctic Service.*

An account of an exploring expedition into the Arctic regions; it reached the northernmost point which at that time had been attained.

Trail and Camp-Fire

PROF. D. G. ELLIOTT. *Monograph of Pittas.*
Monograph of Grouse.
Monograph of Pheasants.
Monograph of Cats.
Monograph of Hornbills.
New and Heretofore Unfigured Birds of North America.
Shore Birds of North America.
Gallinaceous Game Birds of North America.
Wild Animals (Wolf).
Synopsis of the Trochiladæ.

Most of these are sumptuous folios, containing handsome colored plates, with accompanying descriptive texts, of the different mammals or birds in each of the groups dealt with. The shore birds and the gallinaceous game birds are illustrated with uncolored plates.

GEORGE BIRD GRINNELL, PH.D. *Pawnee Hero Stories and Folk Tales.*

The life history and folk lore of the Pawnees, told by one who is himself an adopted member of the tribe. Incidentally there are excellent descriptions of the chase of the bison ; and, except in the volume next mentioned, in no other book can there be found so vivid and accurate an account of the outward and inward life of an Indian tribe.

List of Books

Blackfoot Lodge Tales.

A volume on the same plan, dealing with the Blackfeet, as they were, and as they are; and their methods of warfare and the chase, their life, social organization and religion, and their strange traditions.

The Story of the Indian.

A more general book on the Indians of the West, treating of their home life, their hunting, their wars, their religious beliefs, and finally of some of the changes which came to them with the advent of the white man. In these three volumes an effort is made to treat the native American hunter from a point of view somewhat novel—his own.

CLARENCE KING. *Mountaineering in the Sierra Nevadas.*

Charmingly written chapters on explorations among the Sierras, when they were virgin, and of pioneer trips to the summits of the loftier peaks.

DR. C. HART MERRIAM. *Mammals of the Adirondacks.*

The full life histories of all the mammals, from bear and deer to shrews and meadow-mice, found in the Adirondacks, by a man who is a field naturalist in the highest sense of the term; the model of what we ought to have for the entire American continent.

Trail and Camp-Fire

Hon. Theodore Roosevelt. *The Wilderness Hunter.*

The life of a hunter in the fast-vanishing American wilderness, in the forests, the mountains and the great plains ; and chapters on the chase of every kind of big game characteristic of temperate North America, with horse, hound and rifle. The only book describing the chase of all the big game of the United States, by a man who has himself shot them all; and describing also the wilderness itself, in all its many forms, and the men who dwell and hunt therein.

Hunting Trips of a Ranchman.

Sporting experiences of a cattle ranchman on the northern plains, and accounts of the chase of all the game animals which yield him sport and food.

Ranch Life and the Hunting Trail.

The ranch country, and life among the ranchmen and cowboys; their work and pastimes, their feats with horse and rope and rifle. Also further hunting experiences; the chapter on the bighorn sheep contains the first fairly full account of its life history.

Dean Sage. *The Restigouche and its Salmon Fishing; with a Chapter on Angling Literature.*

A luxurious volume on Canadian salmon angling.

List of Books

FRANCIS PARKMAN. *The California and Oregon Trail.*

An American classic, the best of its kind, and too well known to need more than an allusion.

HON. W. WOODVILLE ROCKHILL. *Through Mongolia and Thibet.*

The journal of a trip to parts of mid-Asia never before traversed by a white man, with very full notes on ethnology and geography. It was this journey which procured for Mr. Rockhill the gold medal of the Royal Geographical Society.

T. S. VAN DYKE. *The Still-Hunter.*

A thorough and exceedingly valuable treatise on the science of still-hunting deer; the only book of the kind; a mine of valuable information.

Game Birds at Home.

An account of the habits and shooting of North American game birds.

CHARLES E. WHITEHEAD. *The Camp-Fires of the Everglades.*

A delightful story of a sojourn in Florida before the war, giving a vivid picture of wild life in a country that once abounded in game. A volume noteworthy for the charm of its style.

341

Trail and Camp-Fire

CASPAR W. WHITNEY. *On Snowshoes to the Barren Grounds.*

> The detailed story of a successful midwinter trip, fraught with severe hardship, after musk ox.

In addition, there are, of course, numerous magazine articles, pamphlets, reports and the like; not to speak of the three books of the Boone and Crockett Club—the present volume and its two predecessors, " American Big Game Hunting," and " Hunting in Many Lands." There are also chapters in such books as the Century Company's "Sport with Gun and Rod" and Scribner's "Outdoor Library."

Constitution of the Boone and Crockett Club

FOUNDED DECEMBER 1887.

Article I.

This Club shall be known as the Boone and Crockett Club.

Article II.

The objects of the Club shall be:

1. To promote manly sport with the rifle.

2. To promote travel and exploration in the wild and unknown, or but partially known, portions of the country.

3. To work for the preservation of the large game of this country, and, so far as possible, to further legislation for that purpose, and to assist in enforcing the existing laws.

4. To promote inquiry into, and to record observations on, the habits and natural history of the various wild animals.

5. To bring about among the members the interchange of opinions and ideas on hunting, travel and exploration; on the various kinds of hunting rifles; on the haunts of game animals, etc.

343

Trail and Camp-Fire

Article III.

No one shall be eligible for regular membership who shall not have killed with the rifle, in fair chase, by still-hunting or otherwise, at least one individual of each of three of the various kinds of American large game.

Article IV.

Under the head of American large game are included the following animals: Black or brown bear, grizzly bear, polar bear, buffalo (bison), mountain sheep, woodland caribou, barren-ground caribou, cougar, musk-ox, white goat, elk (wapiti), pronghorn antelope, moose, Virginia deer, mule deer, and Columbian black-tail deer.

Article V.

The term "fair chase" shall not be held to include killing bear or cougar in traps, nor "fire hunting," nor "crusting" moose, elk or deer in deep snow, nor "calling" moose, nor killing deer by any other method than fair stalking or still-hunting, nor killing game from a boat while it is swimming in the water, nor killing the female or young of any ruminant, except the female of white goat or of musk-ox.

Article VI.

This Club shall consist of not more than one hundred regular members, and of such associate and honorary members as may be elected by the Executive Committee. Associate members shall be chosen

Constitution, Boone and Crockett Club

from those who by their furtherance of the objects of
the Club, or general qualifications, shall recommend
themselves to the Executive Committee. Associate
and honorary members shall be exempt from dues
and initiation fees, and shall not be entitled to vote.

Article VII.

The officers of the Club shall be a President, five
Vice-Presidents, a Secretary, and a Treasurer, all of
whom shall be elected annually. There shall also be
an Executive Committee, consisting of six members,
holding office for three years, the terms of two of
whom shall expire each year. The President, the
Secretary, and the Treasurer, shall be *ex-officio* members of the Executive Committee.

Article VIII.

The Executive Committee shall constitute the
Committee on Admissions. The Committee on Admissions may recommend for regular membership by
unanimous vote of its members present at any meeting, any person who is qualified under the foregoing
articles of this Constitution. Candidates thus recom-
mended shall be voted on by the Club at large. Six
blackballs shall exclude, and at least one-third of the
members must vote in the affirmative to elect.

Article IX.

The entrance fee for regular members shall be
twenty-five dollars. The annual dues of regular

345

members shall be five dollars, and shall be payable on February 1st of each year. Any member who shall fail to pay his dues on or before August 1st, following, shall thereupon cease to be a member of the Club. But the Executive Committee, in their discretion, shall have power to reinstate such member.

Article X.

The use of steel traps; the making of "large bags"; the killing of game while swimming in water, or helpless in deep snow; and the killing of the females of any species of ruminant (except the musk-ox or white goat), shall be deemed offenses. Any member who shall commit such offenses may be suspended, or expelled from the Club by unanimous vote of the Executive Committee.

Article XI.

The officers of the Club shall be elected for the ensuing year at the annual meeting.

Article XII.

This Constitution may be amended by a two-thirds vote of the members present at any annual meeting of the Club, provided that notice of the proposed amendment shall have been mailed, by the Secretary, to each member of the Club, at least two weeks before said meeting.

By-Laws
Rules of the Committee on Admission

1. Candidates must be proposed and seconded in writing by two members of the Club.

2. Letters concerning each candidate must be addressed to the Executive Committee by at least two members, other than the proposer and seconder.

3. No candidate for regular membership shall be proposed or seconded by any member of the Committee on Admissions.

4. No person shall be elected to associate membership who is qualified for regular membership, but withheld therefrom by reason of there being no vacancy.

Additional information as to the admission of members may be found in Articles III, VI, VIII and IX of the Constitution.

Former Officers Boone and Crockett Club

President.

Theodore Roosevelt,	1888-1894.
Benjamin H. Bristow,	1895-1896.
W. Austin Wadsworth,	1897-

Vice-Presidents.

Charles Deering,	1897-
Walter B. Devereux,	1897-
Howard Melville Hanna,	1897-
William D. Pickett,	1897-
Frank Thomson,	1897-1900.
Owen Wister,	1900-1902.
Archibald Rogers,	1903-

Secretary and Treasurer.

Archibald Rogers,	1888-1893.
George Bird Grinnell,	1894-1895.
C. Grant La Farge,	1896-1901.

Secretary.

Alden Sampson,	1902.
Madison Grant,	1903-

Treasurer.

C. Grant La Farge,	1902-

Executive Committee.

W. Austin Wadsworth,	1893-1896.
George Bird Grinnell,	1893.
Winthrop Chanler,	1893-1899, 1904-
Owen Wister,	1893-1896, 1903-
Charles F. Deering,	1893-1896.
Archibald Rogers,	1894-1902.
Lewis Rutherford Morris,	1897-
Henry L. Stimson,	1897-1899.
Madison Grant,	1897-1902.
Gifford Pinchot,	1900-1903.
Caspar Whitney,	1900-1903.
John Rogers, Jr.,	1902-
Alden Sampson,	1903-
Arnold Hague,	1904-

Editorial Committee.

George Bird Grinnell,	1896-
Theodore Roosevelt,	1896-

348

Officers
of the Boone and Crockett Club
1904

President.

W. Austin Wadsworth........Geneseo, N. Y.

Vice-Presidents.

Charles Deering....................Illinois.
Walter B. Devereux..............Colorado
Howard Melville Hanna.............Ohio.
William D. Pickett...............Wyoming.
Archibald Rogers...............New York.

Secretary.

Madison Grant.............New York City.

Treasurer.

C. Grant La Farge.........New York City.

Executive Committee.

W. Austin Wadsworth, *ex-officio*, Chairman,
Madison Grant, *ex-officio*,
C. Grant La Farge, *ex-officio*,

Lewis Rutherford Morris, } To serve until 1905.
John Rogers, Jr., }

Alden Sampson, } To serve until 1906.
Owen Wister, }

Arnold Hague, } To serve until 1907.
Winthrop Chanler, }

Editorial Committee.

George Bird Grinnell............New York.
Theodore Roosevelt......Washington, D. C.

349

List of Members
of the Boone and Crockett Club, 1904

Regular Members.

Major Henry T. Allen,	Washington, D. C.
Col. George S. Anderson,	Washington, D. C.
James W. Appleton,	New York City.
Gen. Thomas H. Barber,	New York City.
Daniel M. Barringer,	Philadelphia, Pa.
F. S. Billings,	Woodstock, Vt.
George Bird,	New York City.
George Bleistein,	Buffalo, N. Y.
W. J. Boardman,	Washington, D. C.
William B. Bogert,	Chicago, Ill.
William B. Bristow,	New York City.
Arthur Erwin Brown,	Philadelphia, Pa.
Capt. Willard H. Brownson,	Washington, D. C.
John Lambert Cadwalader,	New York City.
Royal Phelps Carroll,	New York City.
Winthrop Chanler,	New York City.
William Astor Chanler,	New York City.
Charles P. Curtis, Jr.,	Boston, Mass.
Frank C. Crocker,	Hill City, S. D.
Dr. Paul J. Dashiell,	Annapolis, Md.
E. W. Davis,	New York City.
Charles Stewart Davison,	New York City.
Charles Deering,	Chicago, Ill.

List of Members

HORACE K. DEVEREUX,	Colorado Springs, Col.
WALTER B. DEVEREUX	New York City.
H. CASIMIR DE RHAM,	Tuxedo, N. Y.
DR. WILLIAM K. DRAPER,	New York City.
J. COLEMAN DRAYTON,	New York City.
DR. DANIEL GIRAUD ELLIOT,	Chicago, Ill.
MAJOR ROBERT TEMPLE EMMET,	Schenectady, N. Y.
MAXWELL EVARTS,	New York City.
ROBERT MUNRO FERGUSON,	New York City.
JOHN G. FOLLANSBEE,	New York City.
JAMES T. GARDINER,	New York City.
JOHN STERETT GITTINGS,	Baltimore, Md.
GEORGE H. GOULD,	Santa Barbara, Cal.
MADISON GRANT,	New York City.
DE FOREST GRANT,	New York City.
GEORGE BIRD GRINNELL,	New York City.
WILLIAM MILNE GRINNELL,	New York City.
ARNOLD HAGUE,	Washington, D. C.
HOWARD MELVILLE HANNA,	Cleveland, Ohio.
JAMES HATHAWAY KIDDER,	Boston, Mass.
DR. WALTER B. JAMES,	New York City.
C. GRANT LA FARGE,	New York City.
DR. ALEXANDER LAMBERT,	New York City.
COL. OSMUN LATROBE,	New York City.
GEORGE H. LYMAN,	Boston, Mass.
FRANK LYMAN,	Brooklyn, N. Y.
CHARLES B. MACDONALD,	New York City.
HENRY MAY,	Washington, D. C.
DR. JOHN K. MITCHELL,	Philadelphia, Pa.
J. PIERPONT MORGAN, JR.,	New York City.
J. CHESTON MORRIS, JR.,	Springhouse, Pa.
DR. LEWIS RUTHERFORD MORRIS,	New York City.

351

HENRY NORCROSS MUNN,	New York City.
LYMAN NICHOLS,	Boston, Mass.
THOMAS PATON,	New York City.
HON. BOIES PENROSE,	Washington, D. C.
DR. CHARLES B. PENROSE,	Philadelphia, Pa.
R. A. F. PENROSE, JR.,	Philadelphia, Pa.
COL. WILLIAM D. PICKETT,	Four Bear, Wyo.
HENRY CLAY PIERCE,	New York City.
JOHN JAY PIERREPONT,	Brooklyn, N. Y.
GIFFORD PINCHOT,	Washington, D. C.
JOHN HILL PRENTICE,	New York City.
HENRY S. PRITCHETT,	Boston, Mass.
A. PHIMISTER PROCTOR,	New York City.
PERCY RIVINGTON PYNE,	New York City.
BENJAMIN W. RICHARDS,	Philadelphia, Pa.
DOUGLAS ROBINSON,	New York City.
ARCHIBALD ROGERS,	Hyde Park, N. Y.
DR. JOHN ROGERS, JR.,	New York City.
HON. THEODORE ROOSEVELT,	Washington, D. C.
HON. ELIHU ROOT,	New York City.
BRONSON RUMSEY,	Buffalo, N. Y.
LAWRENCE D. RUMSEY,	Buffalo, N. Y.
ALDEN SAMPSON,	Haverford, Pa.
HON. WILLIAM CARY SANGER,	Sangerfield, N. Y.
PHILIP SCHUYLER,	Irvington, N. Y.
M. G. SECKENDORFF,	Washington, D. C.
DR. J. L. SEWARD,	Orange, N. J.
DR. A. DONALDSON SMITH,	Philadelphia, Pa.
DR. WILLIAM LORD SMITH,	Boston, Mass.
E. LE ROY STEWART,	New York City.
HENRY L. STIMSON,	New York City.
HON. BELLAMY STORER,	Washington, D. C.

List of Members

RUTHERFORD STUYVESANT,	New York City.
LEWIS S. THOMPSON,	Red Bank, N. J.
B. C. TILGHMAN, JR.,	Philadelphia, Pa.
HON. W. K. TOWNSEND,	New Haven, Conn.
MAJOR W. AUSTIN WADSWORTH,	Geneseo, N. Y.
SAMUEL D. WARREN,	Boston, Mass.
JAMES SIBLEY WATSON,	Rochester, N. Y.
CASPAR WHITNEY,	New York City.
COL. ROGER D. WILLIAMS,	Lexington, Ky.
FREDERIC WINTHROP,	New York City.
ROBERT DUDLEY WINTHROP,	New York City.
OWEN WISTER,	Philadelphia, Pa.
J. WALTER WOOD, JR.,	Short Hills, N. J.

Associate Members.

HON. TRUXTON BEALE,	Washington, D. C.
WILLIAM L. BUCHANAN,	Buffalo, N. Y.
D. H. BURNHAM,	Chicago, Ill.
EDWARD NORTH BUXTON,	Knighton, Essex, Eng.
MAJ. F. A. EDWARDS, U. S.	Embassy, Rome, Italy.
A. P. GORDON-CUMMING,	Washington, D. C.
BRIG.-GEN. A. W. GREELY,	Washington, D. C.
MAJOR MOSES HARRIS,	Washington, D. C.
HON. JOHN F. LACEY,	Washington, D. C.
HON. HENRY CABOT LODGE,	Washington, D. C.
A. P. LOW,	Ottawa, Canada.
PROF. JOHN BACH MACMASTER,	Philadelphia, Pa.
DR. C. HART MERRIAM,	Washington, D. C.
HON. FRANCIS G. NEWLANDS,	Washington, D. C.
PROF. HENRY FAIRFIELD OSBORN,	New York City.
HON. GEORGE C. PERKINS,	Washington, D. C.
MAJOR JOHN PITCHER,	Washington, D. C.

HON. REDFIELD PROCTOR,	Washington, D. C.
HON. W. WOODVILLE ROCKHILL,	Washington, D. C.
JOHN E. ROOSEVELT,	New York City.
HON. CARL SCHURZ,	New York City.
F. C. SELOUS,	Worpleston, Surrey, Eng.
T. S. VAN DYKE,	Los Angeles, Cal.
HON. G. G. VEST,	Washington, D. C.

Regular Members, Deceased.

ALBERT BIERSTADT,	New York City.
HON. BENJAMIN H. BRISTOW,	New York City.
H. A. CAREY,	Newport, R. I.
COL. RICHARD IRVING DODGE,	Washington, D. C.
COL. H. C. MCDOWELL,	Lexington, Ky.
MAJOR J. C. MERRILL,	Washington, D. C.
DR. WILLIAM H. MERRILL,	New York City.
JAMES S. NORTON,	Chicago, Ill.
WILLIAM HALLETT PHILLIPS,	Washington, D. C.
N. P. ROGERS,	New York City.
E. P. ROGERS,	New York City.
ELLIOTT ROOSEVELT,	New York City.
DR. J. WEST ROOSEVELT,	New York City.
DEAN SAGE,	Albany, N. Y.
HON. CHARLES F. SPRAGUE,	Boston, Mass.
FRANK THOMSON,	Philadelphia, Pa.
MAJ.-GEN. WILLIAM D. WHIPPLE,	New York City.
CHARLES E. WHITEHEAD,	New York City.

Honorary Members, Deceased.

JUDGE JOHN DEAN CATON,	Ottawa, Ill.
FRANCIS PARKMAN,	Boston, Mass.
GEN. WILLIAM TECUMSEH SHERMAN,	New York City.
GEN. PHILIP SHERIDAN,	Washington, D. C.

List of Members

Associate Members, Deceased.

Hon. Edward F. Beale,	Washington, D. C.
Col. John Mason Brown,	Louisville, Ky.
Major Campbell Brown,	Spring Hill, Ky.
Hon. Wade Hampton,	Columbia, S. C.
Maj.-Gen. W. H. Jackson,	Nashville, Tenn.
Clarence King,	New York City.
Hon. Thomas B. Reed,	New York City.